THE MAN WHO JUMPED OFF CLOUDS

ADVENTURES OF A JUNGLE PILOT

WELLESLEY MUIR

REVIEW AND HERALD® PUBLISHING ASSOCIATION
HAGERSTOWN, MD 21740

This book was
Edited by Gerald Wheeler
Designed by Willie Duke
Electronic makeup by Shirley M. Bolivar
Typeset: 11/12 Bembo

PRINTED IN U.S.A.

04 03 02 01 00   5 4 3 2 1

R&H Cataloging Service
Muir, Wellesley, 1926-
    The man who jumped off clouds.

    1. Peters, Clyde.   2. Missions—Seventh-day
Adventists—Peru.   I. Title.
                [B]

ISBN 0-8280-1441-8

To order additional copies of *The Man Who Jumped Off
Clouds,* by Wellesley Muir, call **1-800-765-6955.**

Visit our Website at *www.rhpa.org* for information on other
Review and Herald products.

THANK YOU!

Evelyn, Gail, and Gladys, my wife and daughters, for reading the manuscript, correcting errors, and making valuable suggestions. Your willingness to live in a tent in the Amazon jungle for four and a half months, while we supervised the construction of the Adventist Mission Air Base in the upper Amazon jungle of Peru, gave our family a chance to see first-hand the beginning of Clyde Peter's aviation ministry with the *Fernando Stahl.*

Clyde Peters, for sharing your adventures for God in reaching Amazon jungle tribes in Peru with the gospel and for taking time from your busy schedule to review the manuscript and make necessary corrections.

Eleanor Peters, for all the help and encouragement you have given Clyde in his work of flying for God and for being the mother of three wonderful children, Shelly, Alan, and Linda. We asked your mother-in-law what she considered her son's greatest accomplishment in life. Without hesitation she replied, "Marrying Eleanor."

Alfredo and Flora Kalbermater and all who worked with you, for the support you gave to the work at the Upper Amazon Mission Air Base. Your dedication to God's service helped make this story possible.

Marvin and Waloma Fehrenbach and Siegfried and Evelyn Nuendorff, for being mission station directors during the early years of the Adventist aviation program and for valuable help reviewing sections of the manuscript involving your mission stations.

James Aitken, Don Christman, and Charles Case, former South American Division, Inca Union, and Upper Amazon Mission presidents, for your vision in promoting an air ministry to reach the tribes of the upper Amazon in Peru.

Jeannette R. Johnson, acquisitions editor, and **Gerald Wheeler,** assistant vice president of editorial (books), for all you have done to help make the publication of this book possible.

Others who read the manuscript and made valuable suggestions include: Justin Bell, Kathy Fagan, Eileen Lantry, Kay Rizzo, Penny Wheeler, and Geraldine Wicks.

And finally, **All Readers** of this book for giving generously to support missions around the world. "The missionary spirit needs to be revived in our churches. Every member of the church should study how to help forward the work of God, both in home missions and in foreign countries" (*Testimonies for the Church,* vol. 6, p. 29).

All royalties from this book are being donated for aviation ministry in the upper Amazon jungle of Peru and for work among Indian tribes who still need to hear the good news that Jesus is coming soon.

DEDICATION

In memory of the late Robert Seamount, a pioneer in mission aviation, and to the tribes of the upper Amazon jungle of Peru.

Aguaruna	**Jebero**
Amahuaca	**Machiguenga**
Amuesha	**Muináni**
Bora	**Murui**
Campa	**Ocaina**
Cashibo	**Piro**
Chayawita	**Shapra**
Cocama	**Shipibo**
Culina	**Ticuna**
Huambisa	**Yagua**
Huarayo	

Amazon Indians donated more than 400,000 hours of labor building about 50 airstrips for Adventist mission planes. Half of this occurred during the first five months of operation. No one knows how many thousands of hours it has taken to maintain the strips. One thing is sure: without these patient jungle people there would have been no mission air ministry. Their labor of love opened doors for mission planes to arrive with the Word of God.

"Then I saw another angel flying in the midst of heaven, having the everlasting gospel to preach to those who dwell on the earth—to every nation, tribe, tongue, and people—saying with a loud voice, 'Fear God and give glory to Him, for the hour of His judgment has come; and worship Him who made heaven and earth, the sea and springs of water'" (Rev. 14:6, 7, NLKV).

WORDS TO UNDERSTAND

AGL: Above ground level

Capitán: Spanish for captain. The people of Peru often call the mission pilot Capitán.

Capwells: Two hinged metal plates near each shoulder on a parachute harness. They must be unsnapped to free a parachutist from the parachute.

Chacra: Spanish for a small family farm or big garden.

¿Como Estás? Spanish question: "How are you?"

Cushma: Campa word for a handwoven cotton robe worn by both men and women in the upper Amazon jungle. The men's robes have vertical stripes while women's robes have horizontal ones.

Fiesta: Spanish for a celebration, usually involving drinking and dancing.

Gringo: A Spanish nickname applied to caucasian foreigners.

Hola: Spanish for "hello."

Machete: A large heavy knife used for cutting underbrush—almost every jungle family owns one.

Mazato: Campa name for a jungle brew with a high alcohol content.

Peckypeck: Word used in the Amazon jungle for a dugout canoe with small inboard motor, usually a Briggs and Stratton with a long, movable shaft and an outboard propeller. The sound of the motor is "peck, peck, peck, peck."

Pistaco: Used in Peru to refer to a fantasized spirit, especially that of a White person, that will cause harm.

Rig: Put in condition for use. A parachute rigger is someone licensed to pack an emergency chute.

Señor: Spanish for Sir or Mr.

Señora: Spanish for Madam or Mrs.

Shushupie: Jungle name for fer-de-lance or pit viper, the most poisonous snake in the Amazon jungle.

Spot: In jumpmaster lingo this means find the ideal spot for a parachute jumper to leave the plane.

Spread eagle: Skydiver's position with legs spread apart and arms out. It keeps the skydiver in a stable position, thus avoiding twisting and turning.

Yarina Cocha: Quechua for Lake of the Palms, site of the Adventist mission air base near the city of Pucallpa in the upper Amazon jungle of Peru.

Yuca: Cassava—a stringy, starchy root grown in the tropics and eaten like potatoes, usually boiled.

CONTENTS

CHAPTER ONE

CHRISTMAS EVE CRASH

Clyde Peters is dead!" the low gravelly voice of Peru's leading news commentator, Juan Ramirez Lazo, bellowed out on the evening news. "This is the latest tragedy in connection with the loss of LANSA Airline flight 508 that crashed in the Amazon jungle 12 days ago. After learning that a 17-year-old girl had survived and reached a woodcutter's cabin 11 days after the accident, North American missionary Clyde Peters parachuted into the crash site to search for more survivors. He hasn't been heard from and is presumed dead."

The news hit like a bolt of lightening. "How can Clyde be dead?" I asked myself. "He's the first fulltime Seventh-day Adventist missionary pilot. Flying the mission plane, *Fernando Stahl*, he takes God's love and last-day three angels message to remote tribes in the upper Amazon jungle. And he's a jump master with nearly 800 jumps recorded in his parachute logbook."

Tormented by questions without answers, I paced the floor while sharp pain stabbed the pit of my stomach. "Why would God allow Clyde to die during an attempt to save human life? Why should a missionary wife like Eleanor have to suffer the loss of her husband? What will the three Peter's children, Shelly, Alan, and Linda, do without a father?"

★ ★ ★

On Christmas Eve Clyde Peters lay in bed burning with fever from a bout with hepatitis. Unable to fly for more than a week, his condition seemed to grow worse. He had no way to know that events earlier that day would plunge him into the greatest predicament of his life.

Before noon on December 24, Juliane Koepcke, blond, barely five feet tall and weighing 90 pounds, boarded LANSA flight 508 headed for the Peruvian city of Pucallpa. The only child of German scientists, she had just graduated from high school in Lima, Peru. She buckled up in a window seat in the third row from the back on the right side of the plane. Her mother, Dr. Marie Koepcke, an ornithologist, sat beside her.

Dr. Marie had recently completed bird drawings for a series of Peruvian stamps. She had delivered her art work in Lima, attended her daughter's graduation, and was now flying home with the girl for the holidays. They would join husband and father, Dr. Hans Koepcke, an ecologist who studied Amazon wild life.

The airliner climbed to 24,000 feet and leveled off. Juliane gazed out at the snow-covered Andes, the peaks reflecting the late-morning sun like giant diamonds. Turning to her mother, she said, "I can't wait to get home to spend Christmas Eve with you and Daddy."

"Now that you're finished with high school, what are your plans for college?" her mother questioned.

"Mom, I've decided to follow your example and study biology."

A holiday atmosphere permeated the plane. Since the school year in Peru begins in April and ends in December, most of the passengers were students heading home for holidays in the jungle. They carried gifts for their parents, brothers, and sisters. Talking and laughter flooded the cabin as everyone anticipated the joy of joining their families at the end of the flight.

After serving snacks, three stewardesses entered the cockpit and started flirting with the pilots. Conversation focused on the crew's Christmas Eve party scheduled for their return to Lima. "Our wives may get a little jealous when they see us dancing and drinking with pretty stewardesses," one of the men joked.

The plane descended to 18,000 feet. Shortly after 12:00 noon, Captain Carlos Forno radioed traffic control. "Estimated arrival in Pucallpa is 12:47 p.m."

A huge black cloud climbed high in their flight path. Jerry Villegas, copilot, shouted at the captain, "Are you going into this?"

"Of course!" The pilot, irritated at being questioned, flew straight ahead into the storm. Heavy rain pounded the plane.

The flight crew joked when two stewardesses left. "Fasten Seat Belt" signs flashed on. Captain Forno called for a reduction in power and reported leaving 18,000 feet. Stewardess Doris Small, still in the cockpit when the plane lurched ahead in terrible turbulence, screamed, "I'm going back to the cabin!"

"No!" the pilot commanded. "Stay where you are and hang on!"

Back in the tail section, Juliane clung to her mother's arm as she watched huge drops of rain beat against the window. A flash of lightning hit the edge of a wing. Baggage flew out of the overhead racks. A woman screamed. Juliane braced herself when a yellow flame leaped across the right wing. Her mother cried, "This is the end of everything!" Then a violent explosion shook the plane.

A noisy crowd waited at the Pucallpa airport for the 1:00 p.m. arrival of LANSA flight 508. Excited families, eager to celebrate, prepared to welcome relatives and friends home for Christmas Eve. Since changing weather often delayed jungle flights, no one showed concern when the plane had not arrived by 1:15 p. m. By 2:00 a rumor circulated that instead of landing in Pucallpa, the plane had flown on to Iquitos, bypassing a severe storm.

Some LANSA Airline employees hauled out a bulletin board and posted a notice: "Official Communication: LANSA Flight 508 Left Lima at 11:38 am. The pilot radioed from over Oyon at 12:09 pm estimating arrival in Pucallpa at 12:47 pm."

The Christmas Eve spirit in the rustic terminal instantly vanished. Eager anticipation turned to anxiety as parents and spouses pressed LANSA agents for more information. All the employees could say was that they didn't know anything. Finally, weary agents closed their doors and refused to talk.

The mayor of Pucallpa, his face drawn, waited with the others. "My two daughters are on the missing flight," he said. "We planned to celebrate tonight. Now without the arrival of flight 508, this could be the worst Christmas in the history of our city." Perplexed people pounded in vain on doors at the LANSA office. Finally they headed home, walking as if in a funeral procession.

Early that evening and unaware of Juliane and the LANSA

flight, the Peters' children crowded around Clyde's bed for worship. Eleanor, sitting near her husband, led them in singing carols. The sounds of "Silent Night" and other favorites drifted out in the warm tropical night. They read from God's Word and talked about the gift of Jesus—"Immanuel, God with us"— a Jesus who came to "save His people from their sins." The children prayed that their father would get well soon.

Clyde, exhausted from the hepatitis, fell asleep early. At 7:00 a. m. on December 25 a loud knock on the front door awakened him. Eleanor led David Aguilar into their bedroom. "Sorry to disturb you so early on Christmas morning," he said.

"It's all right," Clyde responded.

Tears filled David's eyes as he spoke. "LANSA Airline flight 508 with 92 people on board failed to arrive yesterday and is reported missing. Commander Manuel del Carpio is calling for every available airplane to join a search for the missing airliner."

Minutes later, Stan Sornberger charged in with more details. "Five Baptist missionaries were passengers on the missing plane, including a teenager named Nathan Lyons."

In spite of his weakened condition after long days in bed with hepatitis, Clyde forced himself to sit up and started dressing. "I've got to help find the lost plane," he explained to his reluctant family. "I'm praying for survivors, and they will need help."

Calling student missionary Dan Wenberg, Clyde rushed to the hangar to inspect the mission plane, check the oil, and fuel up. "You know, Dan," Clyde confided, "14-year-old Nathan is on that plane. He's about the age of my son, Alan. That boy's fascinated with parachutes, and every time I've jumped, he's been here. His father's a real friend who's helped me many times." Clyde grabbed a couple of parachutes and flew to the Pucallpa airport. There Commander del Carpio, chief search coordinator, marked areas on his map for him to patrol.

With Dan and two other men in his plane to help observe, he began combing the jungle for signs of a crash. As each weary hour passed, Clyde realized more fully that the task of spotting a lost airliner in the immense jungle below would be next to impossible. A sinking sun cast long shadows across the dirt runway when they landed back at the Adventist air base. Exhausted, Clyde climbed out of the plane and stumbled back to his house.

Eleanor hugged her tired husband and after serving him a good meal, put him to bed. "Today I read an article in *Life and*

Health magazine describing a treatment for infectious hepatitis," she commented. "I want to give it a try." She followed the recommendations for hot and cold compresses over the liver area. The hydrotherapy began to relieve Clyde's discomfort.

He slept all night and she gave him another treatment the next morning. Before flying out, he smiled at her. "You're the best wife in the world. I can't believe something so simple as hot and cold water could make me feel so much better."

He kept searching, though every four or five hours he would fly home where Eleanor would give him another treatment. Then feeling better, he would take off again. Each day his health improved. "Thank You, Lord," he prayed, "but why does every day end without any sign of the LANSA plane?"

After seven days the Peruvian Air Force called off the search. Because the German embassy in Lima wanted Dr. Hans Koepcke to get official word that his wife, Maria, and daughter, Juliane, were on the missing plane, Clyde flew to the jungle farm where Dr. Koepcke conducted scientific studies. Peters tried to encourage the scientist. "Until the plane is found, there's still hope of survivors," he suggested.

The scientist snarled at the idea of finding anyone alive. "The plane crashed. My wife and daughter are dead. That's it!"

"You can believe as you wish doctor, but I'm praying survivors will be found. Even though the search has officially ended, I'll keep right on looking." Clyde waved as the mission plane lifted off the jungle farm. No one knew that four days later Dr. Koepcke would get the surprise of his life.

After hearing a terrible explosion on the Christmas Eve flight, Juliane watched the right wing rip away from the plane at about 10,000 feet elevation. Seconds later she found herself flying *outside* the plane, still strapped to her seat. As she tumbled, twisted, and twirled, falling at 120 miles an hour, she asked herself, *Am I dreaming? Can this be real?*

Far below she saw jungle treetops. *They look like cauliflowers,* she thought. Her eyes watered as wind swished by, blurring her vision. Everything went black. When she awoke, she hung upside down still strapped in the triple seat. The two seats next to her were empty. There was no sign of her mother or the other passenger. She looked at her watch. "Four o'clock."

Three hours had passed since the airliner disintegrated in a violent thunderstorm. The only sounds now were croaking frogs and pouring rain. Miraculously, the branches of tall jungle trees broke her fall. One swollen eye made it difficult to see. She felt a bump on her head and saw a gash on one foot. In addition, she had a cut on her right arm and a broken collar bone, yet she felt no pain.

Although she managed to unbuckle her seat belt and get to the ground, she didn't have enough energy to leave the area of trees. Suffering shock and half asleep, she spent the whole night lying under the seat, trying to protect herself from heavy rain.

The next morning Juliane awoke to the songs of jungle birds. Huge green trees screened the sunlight. Slowly she crawled out from under the seats. After taking a few steps, she found a small package and opened it. It contained fruitcake and hard candy. When she bit into the fruitcake, soaked from rain, it tasted terrible and she threw it away, but took the wrapped candy. Hoping to avoid poisonous snakes, she picked up a long stick to probe any ground covered with vegetation.

During her years living with her parents in the jungle she learned that it's not big animals, such as jaguars, that are dangerous. It's the small ones—snakes, spiders, poisonous insects, and perhaps worst of all, malaria-infested mosquitos. Poking along with her stick, she looked for her mother. *What's wrong with me?* Feeling dizzy, she stopped to rest.

"Mother! Mother!" she called. No one answered. Then she followed a swarm of flies to a row of airplane seats. Flies buzzed around the motionless bodies of three girls still held by their seat belts. Sickened by this scene of death, Juliane moved on.

After searching for hours she stopped dead still. *What's that?* She listened to the gentle sound of a small stream and remembered the words of her parents. "Juliane, if you ever get lost in the jungle, find a stream and follow it. It will lead to a larger stream. Rivers are the roads for the Indians and plantation people who live along their banks. Eventually you'll get back to civilization."

She understood some of the hazards of traveling jungle waterways. Rivers meander around so much that one can go for hours and advance only a few hundred yards. Piranhas, fish with razor-like teeth, could be attracted by blood from the gash on her foot and tear away her flesh in seconds. At night millions of malaria-infested mosquitos swarm the river banks.

Juliane had boarded the plane wearing white shoes with

high heels. One was gone when she woke up on the jungle floor and she had thrown the other one away. Barefoot, she tried to follow the riverbank, but the thick tangle of jungle vines made each step difficult. Often she had to wade in the water. At night, blood-thirsty mosquitos attacked her. The itching from hundreds of bites made sleep impossible. In the daytime large flies kept stinging and laying eggs in the open sores on her arm and foot.

Occasionally she heard aircraft engines and thought, *They're searching for the plane.* She knew they could never see her through the dense canopy of jungle trees, yet she looked up and screamed. "Hello! Help! Help!" Soon the sound of the engines would fade away. *I'm alone again, but I can't get discouraged. At least I've been able to find small streams with clear water to drink, and I don't feel hungry.*

On the third day vultures circled overhead and she guessed they indicated the presence of dead bodies in the area. Stumbling to a piece of the plane's fuselage, she found no sign of survivors. Baked by suffocating jungle heat, she staggered on. The river widened and even though she feared being eaten by piranhas, she risked swimming whenever possible. Trying to sleep in wet clothes at night, she listened to the haunting sounds of predators in search of a meal.

Finally, on the fourth day, she ate the last of her candy and considered eating some toads, but decided against it. She resisted eating wild fruit since many jungle plants are poisonous. Seeing maggots crawling in her wounds, she imagined, *I'm being eaten alive!* The eggs laid by flies were beginning to hatch.

The river grew wider and wilder. Juliane swam more often, always trying to avoid logjams, rapids, and whirlpools. Each time it looked safe ahead, she swam. When she tried to walk, the loss of energy from lack of food, sleepless nights, and humid heat brought pain to each barefoot step.

Late on the tenth day she caught sight of a dugout canoe tied to a tree in front of her. *Someone lives here!* she wanted to shout. Limping along a narrow path, she reached a small weather-beaten thatched hut. "Hello, hello!" she called. Although she received no response, the door stood open. Entering cautiously, she found a small outboard motor and a can of gasoline sitting on the rough wood floor. *Wonderful—people do live here! I hope they come back soon.*

As she collapsed on the floor she wondered, *What will happen if the owners come back and find me asleep?* Screaming parakeets and howler monkeys didn't keep her from falling asleep, though. When she awoke in the morning to the sound of a torrential rain her first thought was about the canoe. *I could take it and go on down the river. No! That's stealing, and I've never stolen anything in my life.*

While waiting inside the dimly lit hut for the rain to stop, she took a sliver of palm wood and carefully extracted 11 maggots from her infected sores. *Voices! I hear voices!* Three men rushed in out of the rain. Seeing the blond teenage girl with short hair and bangs, they stopped in shock. One asked in Spanish, "What do we have here?"

The muscular *mestizos,* (a mixture of Indian and Spanish) worked as woodcutters, but had gone off to hunt. They knew about the airplane crash and listened to Juliane's story. Gently, they poured kerosene over her infected wounds and extracted another 30 wiggly maggots. Knowing the girl had to be hungry, they prepared food and offered it to her. She couldn't eat at first and laughed, "I guess my stomach's shrunk."

As soon as the rain let up, the men helped Juliane into the canoe, attached the motor, and took her down the Shebonya River. She watched the river grow wider, swifter, and more dangerous. *Could I have made this by myself?* she wondered as the canoe descended wild rapids and dodged whirlpools. Several hours later they beached the canoe at the Amazon settlement of Tournavista.

The staff of a small clinic checked her bloodshot eyes and swollen face. They treated the open lesions on her arms and legs where 41 worms had been removed. Then they arranged for a small plane to fly her to the Summer Institute of Linguistics base at Yarina Cocha where an American missionary doctor could treat her.

After falling 10,000 feet from an exploding plane, 17-year-old Juliane had walked 10 days alone in the jungle. On the eleventh day kind woodcutters took her back to civilization. At the base she asked for a Bible. *Why am I alive?* she wondered. *What plans does God have for me? Why did so many others die?*

News of his daughter's survival reached Dr. Koepcke. Clyde, completing 11 days of searching, arrived back at the base. Hearing how Juliane had walked out of the jungle alive, he rushed over to the Linguistic Base for a visit. He found the girl distressed at the loss of her mother, but absolutely delighted to be with her father.

Dr. Koepcke, who four days earlier declared there was no hope, stood with his arm around his daughter. "What do you think of a brave girl who survives a Christmas Eve crash and then walks alone for 10 tortuous days in wild jungle?" he asked Clyde.

"I think she's great, Doctor, and if there's one survivor, there have to be more. I'll do anything to find anyone still alive and needing help."

The next morning at 5:30 Clyde flew to Puerto Inca with two parachutes in the back of his plane. The authorities were organizing a new search, and a Peruvian Air Force helicopter stood by. More planes arrived, and the pilots studied their maps. With information from Juliane they quickly pinpointed the crash sight to an area of about 20 square miles. The pilots wanted to find the wreckage as soon as possible.

Clyde approached Commander Manuel del Carpio. "If this girl walked away from the crash, there must be more people who are still alive."

Commander del Carpio nodded. "Yes, I've been thinking the same thing."

"If we could get in right away and cut down some trees, helicopters could land. We might find 20 or 30 people still alive."

The officer shook his head. "There's no way we can do that. We don't have anyone prepared to jump into the jungle."

"I can," Clyde volunteered. "I've got all the equipment in the back of my plane right now."

"Really! If that's the case, why don't you get ready? We'll have you jump just as soon as we get word on the location of the crash."

Racing back to his plane, Clyde pulled out his parachute and all the other equipment he would need except for a chain saw. Borrowing a brand new one, he promised to return it before the day was over. Then he spent an hour getting everything tied to his parachute harness. Less than two weeks had passed since he had left his sick bed with hepatitis. After wearing 200 pounds of equipment for 30 minutes, he felt extremely tired and took it off.

The authorities advised the search planes that Peters stood by ready to jump as soon as they spotted the wrecked plane. While waiting, Clyde talked with the helicopter pilot and finalized on the signals they would use.

A plane landed and the pilot ran up. "You'd better hurry, Clyde! I just spotted the LANSA crash. The jungle hides it so well you barely see it. Grab your equipment, and I'll go with you in the helicopter."

Peters considered running back to his plane to pick up the compass he had left on the seat. *Oh, well, I won't need it,* he thought. *I'll cut down a few trees, the helicopter will land, and I'll be back in time for lunch.* He buckled his parachute harness. A provisional knot would hold the chain saw by his side until after the parachute opened. Then he would untie it and release a coil of rope, allowing the saw to drop below him so it would hit the ground first and not injure him.

He climbed into the Alouette helicopter with the chain saw on his left, a large duffle bag on his right, and other items strung over his body. The craft lifted off on a heading of 285°. A United States Air Force Hercules C-130, flown in from Panama, fixed a scope on the wrecked plane and circled around it. The helicopter pilot followed its instructions: "Go right, turn left, you passed it. Turn around and come back."

In spite of the help of the C-130's technology, the helicopter circled 15 minutes before they actually saw the wreckage hidden beneath the vast canopy of green jungle. The chopper climbed to 3,000 feet. The second time around, Clyde prepared to jump, but lost sight of the debris and asked the pilot to circle again.

The third time around he spotted the wreckage, but it disappeared before he could crawl out the open door. Confident of the exact crash location, he jumped anyway. Slowly counting to five, he pulled his rip cord. The candy-striped parachute opened with a jerk. As it did, the chain saw at his side slipped away from its line, dropping like an arrow toward the dense jungle below.

CHAPTER TWO

SKYLINE ROAD

Growing up in northwest Kansas, Clyde had learned to work at an early age. When he wasn't working, he loved being with his old horse Jack and riding bareback. Jack never won ribbons at the county fair, but he didn't need to. The creature was the most faithful, gentle workhorse any farm family could ever own. Clyde's parents, Melvin and Georgianna Peters, labored long hours on their 1,500 acre wheat ranch to provide for Clyde and his older sister, Joyce.

Late one lazy summer afternoon, Clyde climbed off old Jack and sat on a bale of hay, watching a red-tailed hawk riding an updraft. *When I grow up, I'll fly like a hawk. I might even jump off a cloud.*

"Clyde. Hey, Clyde! It's milking time." Dad's voice interrupted the boy's daydreams.

"I'm coming, Dad." Reluctantly he headed toward the big barn. Hoofs pounded the cement as cows walked into their stanchions. As Dad started the milking, Clyde measured out oats and barley for each animal.

After he had the milking machines hooked up, Dad walked over and patted his son on the shoulder. "Sure appreciate your help, son. Some day you'll run this farm. The cows will be yours. Fifteen hundred acres will be a great inheritance. Oh, your sister Joyce will get her share, but you're the one to work this farm."

The boy stared into the soft brown eyes of the family's favorite Jersey cow, then reached out and scratched her face. "You're lucky. You've had all that good hay, and I brought

21

your dessert. How do you like your barley and oats?"

Clyde moved on to the next stanchion. *Dad wants me to grow up and run the farm. What I want to do is fly—I'll travel through the sky like a bird.*

Classes at the little country school in Edson, Kansas, didn't always interest Clyde. It was World War II and stories of paratroopers jumping behind enemy lines fired his imagination. Riding home from school one spring afternoon, Clyde looked at a book with pictures of men parachuting. *That's what I want to do!* He jumped off the yellow school bus and raced to the house.

His mom, busy in the kitchen, didn't notice when he sneaked into the closet and hurried outside with her new black silk umbrella, opening and closing it as he ran. *This will make a great parachute.* Finding a ladder, he climbed up on the chicken house. Cautiously he looked over the edge from the top of the gabled roof and took a deep breath. *It's a long way to the ground!*

As he crawled to the lower edge, he told himself, *Nothing will happen. My parachute's already open.* Clinging to the umbrella, he leaped away from the roof. Scared chickens scrambled in every direction. Suddenly the umbrella turned inside out and Clyde fell like a rock, hitting the ground hard.

When he looked at the umbrella he saw that the hinged ribs were bent and the fabric was torn. *Dad will get me for this!*

Legs hurting, he stood and limped away to hide the umbrella until he could put it back where he found it. A week later Georgianna Peters discovered the damage and told her husband. He waited until supper time for a talk with his son.

"Clyde, do you know anything about your mother's umbrella?"

"Yes, Dad, it's in the closet."

"I know where it is, son, but it's broken. Do you know anything about that?"

"I couldn't help it. I used it and . . . well, . . . you see, it just turned inside out and I fell on top of it—I don't know how to fix it."

"Clyde, this jumping has to stop before you break your neck. Our hired man saw you jump off the chicken house roof."

"I'm sorry, Dad."

"I'm glad you didn't break any bones." Melvin Peters looked at his boy. "You are never to do this again. Although you're only a kid, I've been letting you drive the tractor. I want you to tend to business and grow up to run this farm."

The next February turned bitterly cold. The heaviest snowstorm in years created an emergency at the Peters' farm. Esther Elliot, the wife of their hired hand, went into labor. Huge snow drifts blocked all roads for miles around. No vehicle could get Mrs. Elliot to the hospital.

But the fierce winds blew most of the snow off a newly planted wheat field near the house, giving Mrs. Peters an idea. Georgianna phoned her cousin, Watson, who managed the local airport and owned his own plane. "Could you fly in, pick up a patient, and take her to the hospital?"

"More bad weather is on the way," he said, "but I think I can make it if I hurry."

Clyde watched Watson circle the farm and land his Piper Cub in the wheat field. Esther Elliot's husband helped her into the backseat and the plane took off. She arrived at the hospital in time to give birth to a healthy baby. *Wow! Look what an airplane can do*, Clyde thought. *I'll be a pilot and help people like this.*

One day Mrs. Peters found a coupon advertising the Junior Voice of Prophecy Bible Correspondence Course and showed it to Clyde. He looked it over and said, "Sure, Mom, I'll study these lessons." He mailed the coupon and the lessons began arriving from Los Angeles.

One lesson called attention to the fourth commandment: "Remember the Sabbath day, to keep it holy. Six days you shall labor and do all your work, but the seventh day is the Sabbath of the Lord your God. . . . For in six days the Lord made the heavens and the earth, the sea, and all that is in them, and rested the seventh day (Ex. 20:8-11). Clyde read more: "This is love, that we walk according to His commandments" (2 John 6).

He took the lesson to the kitchen where his mother worked preparing a meal. "Mom, they're asking what I want to do about keeping the Sabbath. What shall I say?"

She hesitated a minute. "Just tell them you're thinking about it." Bible-believing Baptists, Georgianna and Melvin did a lot of thinking too. After attending evangelistic meetings in a tent, Clyde, at 13, and his family were baptized into the Goodland, Kansas, Seventh-day Adventist church.

The new religion emphasized Christian education and Clyde went to study at Campion Academy, where he worked on the school farm. He returned home every summer to help his parents. At 16 he got his own car. After working all day on the farm, he would drive to the Goodland Airport and wash airplanes to earn extra money. *I'll learn to fly and become a crop duster,* he decided.

Without telling his parents, he invested every dollar he earned in flying lessons. Realizing that he couldn't keep it secret forever, he finally spoke with his father. "You need to know, Dad, that I'm taking flight instruction. I plan to be a pilot."

Melvin Peters winced. "What shall I do with a son who doesn't want to farm?"

Georgianna, hearing the conversation, asked, "How can you possibly think of making flying a career?"

Back in academy for his senior year, Clyde worked three hours a day as monitor in the boy's dorm. His best grades were in math and mechanics. Religious things interested him and he got fair grades in Bible. When it came to English and history, however, it was passing grades only. At graduation, Clyde listened to every word of H.M.S. Richards, Sr.'s message, "The Skyline Road."

Only weeks after graduation, he hit his own Skyline Road in his first solo flight. Wheat fields stretched out to the horizon in every direction. His own hands held the controls of the little yellow Champion airplane. Relaxing, he leaned back in the pilot's seat, listening to the steady roar of the engine. *This is what I've longed for—soaring like a bird. Soon I'll have a pilot's license. My life work will revolve around flying.*

CHAPTER THREE

JUMP MASTER

The new pilot's license in his billfold, Clyde sat at the table with his parents enjoying his mom's cooking. His mother, a registered nurse, commented, "You know, Clyde, I think you ought to go to Union College. Anyone who wants to get ahead needs a college education."

At first Clyde wanted to say no, but an idea exploded in his mind. *There's a top aviation school in Lincoln, Nebraska.* "If that's what you want me to do, I'll give college a try."

His dad made it clear, however, that "You'll have to work and do your part, but we will make sure your school bills get paid. All other expense will be up to you."

Clyde drove to Union College and registered for fall classes. Without telling his parents, he also signed up for flight training at Lincoln Aviation. He got a job at college to help pay school expenses there and worked mixing cement for a construction company to cover the aviation courses. Letters from home cautioned: "Don't waste too much time flying."

Early in his sophomore year Clyde began thinking, *I'm too busy! All I do is work, fly, and attend classes.* But he wasn't too busy to notice a brown-eyed brunette from Montana. He talked to Eleanor between classes, asking one day, "How would you like to go flying with me?"

She guessed he had arranged for a pilot to fly them and smiled, "Sounds like fun, I've never been in an airplane. Sure, I'll go." At the airport, Clyde led Eleanor to a Cessna he had rented. "You're a pilot?" she asked.

For a moment she hesitated before letting him help fasten her seat belt. The two took off into a blue sky dotted with puffs of white clouds—a gorgeous day, but the kind of weather that produces a bumpy ride. Terrified by the rough air, Eleanor grabbed Clyde's arm and hung on during the entire flight.

A new idea lodged in Clyde Peters' head. *Eleanor Mae Larson—God made her just for me!* He wrote about her to his parents. "I met Eleanor Larson here at Union College. She's different than the other girls. I'd like to bring her home some weekend." The Peters liked Eleanor, but since their son was only a sophomore, they decided not to encourage the friendship. But he didn't need their approval.

One day the couple started talking about Clyde's interest in flying. "If you like to fly, Clyde, I think that's what you ought to do."

"Thank you, Eleanor! I wish my folks would encourage me like that."

Clyde scraped up enough money to buy an interest in an old Taylor Craft and flew it for 500 hours before selling out and buying an interest in another plane. He continued to attend college classes, but seldom took time to study.

After two years at Union, he went home to spend another summer working on the farm with his parents. "Two things are tearing me apart," he confessed to them. "I love you, Mom and Dad. You need my help, but I'd sure rather be flying. And Eleanor's 700 miles away helping her sister haul hay on her dad's farm."

Melvin Peters looked at his restless son. "Clyde, it sounds like you're thinking about a trip to Montana. We've got a lot of field work to do here, and it has to be done before you go anywhere. You'll take over this farm someday, but you need to learn now that there are times when you just can't leave."

At the end of a hard day, Clyde dialed Eleanor's number. When she answered, he blurted out, "Eleanor, will you marry me?"

She laughed. "Clyde! What are you saying?"

Boy, she doesn't seem excited about this, he thought, but he continued. "Eleanor, I just bought you a new sewing machine."

Now he wanted to see her more than ever. A few days later he purchased new tires for his old Ford and left before dawn the next morning. Arriving late that evening, he leaped up on the porch of the Larson home two steps at a time and knocked. His heart beat fast when Eleanor opened the door. He stared at her. *Are my eyes playing tricks?* "Eleanor, you look just like an angel!"

The Larson's appreciated Clyde's help around the farm, but he could spend only a few days. "Eleanor," he said one day, "why don't you come home with me and get better acquainted with my parents?"

They drove south out of Montana and on through Wyoming. The carburetor acted up and he spent $20 for repairs. At the next service station, he filled the tank. After counting his change, he said, "We've got exactly 29¢ to get us back to my folks."

When he turned the ignition key the car wouldn't start. "This is disgusting!" Raising the hood, he worked on the engine. "The money I spent hasn't helped a bit." When his car finally started, he floor-boarded the throttle and peeled rubber all the way out to the highway. He kept going wide open.

Two miles out a flashing red light appeared in the rearview mirror. The highway patrol signaled him to pull over. *All I have is 29¢ and that won't pay a fine.* Clyde worried, *They'll haul me off to jail for going over the speed limit. What will Eleanor think of me now?*

Then he remembered another complication—an empty whiskey bottle lay on the back seat. Although he didn't drink, he had found the whiskey bottle in a trash can and put it on the rear seat, curious to see his parents reaction when he got home. Now he realized that his practical joke would get him into trouble. When the officer reached the car he glanced at the backseat. "Young man, follow me to the police station."

"Eleanor, how could I ever be so ridiculous?" Clyde clenched the steering wheel. "The police will never believe me."

Entering the police headquarters by himself, he faced the officers. "I know I should never break the speed limit. I got caught drinking in high school and promised never to drink again, and I've kept that promise. I shouldn't torment my parents, but I found a whiskey bottle and put it on the backseat to see how they'd react."

The highway patrolman had watched Clyde's driving all the way to the police station. "I'm convinced he's telling the truth," he commented. Since the young man had no alcohol on his breath, the other police agreed. "Go home, drive carefully, and do all you can to help your folks."

Clyde ran back to the car, and feeling playful in his relief that he wasn't in trouble, he said with a straight face, "Eleanor, they're sending me to jail because I don't have money to pay the fine."

"If that has to be, we'll just make the best of it."

Eleanor looked so kind and spoke so softly that he felt bad for teasing. But her understanding attitude made Clyde all the more positive that *She's the one to be my wife.* Fortunately, the tank of gasoline took them all the way to the Peters' farm.

Wheat harvest had barely ended when wedding bells rang at the little Seventh-day Adventist Church in Goodland. As the wedding march began, Clyde looked down the aisle: *She's got to be the loveliest bride in the world!* Eleanor had clung to Clyde on their first airplane ride together. Now they promised to cling to each other as long as life would last.

Although disappointed that their son would jump into a marriage with no financial resources, Clyde's parents offered to help the newlyweds. "You can live in the little house next to ours where hired help have stayed. Eleanor is a good wife for you, Clyde, and we want you both to get off to a good start. We'll pay you for your work. Later you can take over the farm."

The new husband discussed another decision with Eleanor. "I still own an interest in the plane back in Lincoln. It won't do me any good here in Kansas, so I'm going to sell it."

When he talked about the possibility of getting another plane, Eleanor, knowing how important flying was to her husband, said, "Sure, I think you ought to do it."

With his wife's encouragement, he borrowed money and bought an old junker, then spent a great deal of time overhauling the engine, replacing parts, and patiently painting it to perfection. It gave him practical experience in airplane repair. Afterward he flew it 700 hours before trading it in on a better one.

About a year later, Shelly was born. At the end of the next year the couple had a son, Alan. "You're such a good mother, Eleanor. If I'm going to support my family, I can't be satisfied just flying. I need advanced training in aviation mechanics."

Together they walked over to Clyde's parents' home. "Dad, I appreciate all you and Mom have done for us. This will hurt," he began, "but there's no other way. We've decided to move to Lincoln. If I'm going to be a professional pilot, I need more training."

Melvin Peters' dream for his son to take over the farm evaporated. "OK," he leaned back in his old chair. "If that's what you want, your mother and I won't stop you."

"I'll sure miss having my grandchildren next door," Georgianna added.

Clyde Peters found a job flying a crop duster for the University of Nebraska's Department of Agriculture and enrolled at the Lincoln School of Aviation Mechanics. His difficult experience rebuilding an old plane and making it fly provided incentive, and he learned quickly.

While he worked and studied, Eleanor cared for their growing family. Soon after Clyde's twenty-third birthday, they had a third child, Linda. Another mouth to feed created a need for additional family finances.

One Sunday the head of the local Parachute Club approached him. "We'll pay you to take jumpers up."

"Today I earned money hauling sky divers," he told Eleanor at home that night. "My plane is too small to carry a jump master so they're teaching me to *spot* so I can take beginning jumpers."

"What do you mean, *spot*? She asked.

"I have to calculate wind velocity and direction, then fly the plane to the most ideal location for the parachute student to jump and land on target."

Each time someone jumped from his plane, Clyde thought, *I've got to try this*. While Eleanor encouraged her husband's flying, parachuting troubled her. "Why would the father of three children want to jump out of a plane?" she asked him.

Clyde approached the most qualified parachute instructor in the area. "Say, Shorty, how about training me to be a sky diver?" The tough training began immediately and it came easy for a young man who kept himself physically fit.

He didn't tell Eleanor his first jump was scheduled for the next Sunday. Although he could hardly wait—yet he almost wished Sunday would never come. But early Sunday morning he left home quietly and drove to the airport.

"This is the day I've been waiting for," he greeted his instructor.

"Clyde, be sure to head into the wind," Shorty cautioned, "and judge carefully where you will land. There's more wind than I like, but you'll do OK. You've watched so many people jump, you know a lot more about it than most beginners."

Peters arranged for a friend to fly his plane. Jump master Shorty would stay on the ground. "Clyde, you've spotted for many jumpers. Now you can spot for yourself," he said before the plane took off.

Slipping into the parachute harness, Clyde pulled up the saddle and leg straps, and snapped the D rings. He checked to make sure the leg straps were tight. Finally he fastened on the reserve chute. Shorty watched him climb into the back of the plane and hook up his own static line. "After you leave the plane, count to five. If the static line hasn't opened your parachute, pull the rip cord. If your 'chute doesn't open, use the reserve."

The tiny plane circled to gain altitude while Clyde sat in silence. *Why am I jumping anyway?* Wind speed at ground level had already passed two miles an hour over the maximum of 10 for first-time jumpers. Reaching 3,500 feet AGL (above ground level) gave Clyde time for serious thought. *I didn't tell Eleanor or my children. If the 'chute fails to open I'll sure wish I had.*

The pilot made the final approach into the wind over the target and up wind about the right distance to where the parachute should bring him back to his target. Cautiously Peters crawled out onto the strut. His mind grew numb when he looked down. *Why am I betting my life on a piece of nylon?*

Letting go, he felt as if his stomach had just jumped to his throat. Clyde moved to the spread eagle position, holding his hands and feet out wide to prevent spinning and rolling. *Did I count to five?* he wondered as he fell.

A good solid jerk and the parachute burst open. Sunlight flooded the candy-striped canopy. *This is another world,* he thought as he looked at the lush farms below. *I wish this peace and quiet could last forever.*

Looking down, he suddenly realized, *The real world is coming up fast!* Ground wind had increased and he was off target by a third of a mile. *I'm flying across the ground.* Glancing ahead, he spotted a barbed wire fence! *Wow! I'd better land on this side! No, I can't, I'm already on the other side!*

As he turned into the wind, it swept him up a slope and over a little hill. Boom! He hit hard. The wind blowing at 20 miles an hour pulled him forward, slamming his helmet into the ground. The parachute, filling with air like the sail of a ship, started dragging him. When he struggled to get up and run, the wind pulled him down nose first into the dirt.

Finally he grabbed the bottom shroud line and the parachute collapsed. Clyde sat there on the hard ground, his head aching. *Man, this is a lot tougher than I expected!*

Shorty ran up. "Clyde! Are you OK?"

"Yeah. I'm ready to jump again."

The man glared at him. "Not with this kind of wind. No more jumping today!"

Clyde waited until after his third jump before telling Eleanor. He determined to become a jump master which demanded a D license. Since it required 200 jumps, including 10 from 18,000 feet with a 45 second delay, he parachuted at every opportunity. Several young men in the Lincoln area started a race to see who would be first to complete the requirements.

Friends rooted for Clyde. In one day he jumped 41 times. For his winning jump he parachuted into a lake. He managed to get out with the chute and Shorty signed his log book. The D license came in the mail from the Parachute Club of America, making him the one hundred and seventy-eighth person in the United States to become a jump master.

A few weeks later he received his A & E (aircraft and engine) airplane mechanic's license. He continued earning money hauling jumpers in his own plane and adding more licenses. While flying and jumping were always exciting, Clyde dreamed of doing more. *Where am I going with my life?* he questioned.

Finally he talked it over with Eleanor. "If I had a good job, Dad wouldn't be so determined for me to return to the Kansas farm. I wish I could work for an airline or fly for a corporation."

As a skilled pilot, he received top recommendations from Lincoln Aviation and the University of Nebraska. Yet, every time a good job came up, someone else got hired because he always made it clear, "I don't make commercial flights on Saturday, my Sabbath."

CHAPTER FOUR

AMAZON SIDE OF THE ANDES

One Saturday night at Union College, Clyde, Eleanor, and their children sat watching a South American mission movie. They cringed at the sight of patients being treated for a horrible skin disease called savage fire. A Campa witch doctor in the Amazon jungle gave orders to kill two small girls. At the witch doctor's command, the home where the girls lived exploded in flames. Angered, Clyde asked, "How could anyone be so cruel?"

Impressed with the tremendous needs of remote areas where superstition still ruled, he contacted James J. Aitken, president of the South American Division, and learned that it needed a missionary pilot. After consulting with Eleanor, he applied for the job. "My chances are slim," Clyde told his family. "I have only two years of college, but I'd love to fly for God and help take the gospel of Jesus to the jungle tribes."

"You know," Eleanor said after listening to her husband, "if this is God's plan for us, I believe He will work it out."

Officials at Seventh-day Adventist church world headquarters reviewed Clyde Peters' qualifications. At 26 his flight log recorded more than 3,000 hours in single and multi-engine planes and helicopters. He held a string of licenses, including air-frame, power-plant, single engine land and sea, multi-engine land, commercial helicopter, and flight instructor multi-engine land and sea. He was also a licensed jump master and parachute rigger.

Each day for weeks Clyde checked the mail. "Nothing's arrived from the General Conference," he told Eleanor. "I might as well face the fact. The church isn't interested in using me."

Then one day Eleanor answered the phone, "Clyde, it's for you."

Her husband took the receiver. "Mr. Peters, my company's checked your qualifications and we want to offer you the position of copilot and mechanic on a DC-3. We'll write in your contract that you get Saturdays off, and within two years you'll be promoted to head pilot."

Clyde finished the phone conversation and turned to his wife. "The attractive salary they're promising makes this a very tempting offer."

"But, Clyde, we've prayed about going to South America."

"I know, Eleanor. We better wait until we get some kind of word from the General Conference before I commit to take this job."

At last a letter arrived from church headquarters. "Look, Eleanor!" He tore it open. "Here's an official call for me to serve as the church's first full-time missionary pilot."

"Where do they want us to go?"

"They want me to fly the mission plane, *Fernando Stahl,* in the upper Amazon jungle of Peru."

"God is answering our prayers, Clyde. He's been guiding all along, getting us ready for this."

"Eleanor, we'll be partners with God's three angels to take the everlasting gospel to jungle tribes. I wonder what my parents will say about me flying for God?"

At the Angwin Airport, near the campus of Pacific Union College, 89-year-old Anna Stahl smashed a bottle of orange juice over the nose of the mission plane named in honor of her late husband, pioneer missionary F. A. Stahl. Pastor Bill Baxter, who flew his own private plane in mission service at Montemorelos, Mexico, offered the dedicatory prayer.

James J. Aitken handed the plane's keys to Clyde Peters. "Since you haven't learned Spanish yet and have never made an international flight, we've arranged for a Spanish-speaking pilot, Don Weber, to fly with you to Lima, Peru."

Clyde spent the next two weeks preparing for the 5,000 mile flight. He picked Don Weber up in San Antonio, Texas, and flew on to Brownsville. Before sunrise the next morning, they made a preflight check and radioed the tower for clearance to take off. "Lord, send your angels with the *Fernando Stahl* on it's flight to South America," Peters prayed.

Low clouds on the morning of the second day out required low altitude flying as the men headed south from Vera Cruz on the Gulf of Mexico with plans to reach San Salvador. Before crossing mountains to Tehuantepec on the Pacific, they flew up a valley. Clouds ahead dropped like a curtain all the way down on the rugged terrain.

With zero visibility ahead, Clyde put the plane into a 180° turn, flew back, and landed at a jungle airstrip he had seen earlier. Six men on horses, carrying submachine guns, galloped toward them and stopped in front of the plane. Clyde looked into a barrage of guns aimed at them. "Don, is this what it's like to be a missionary pilot?"

The gunmen didn't understand Clyde's English so Don Weber took over: "We are missionaries on our way to Peru. Bad weather forced us to land."

The men lowered their guns. The pilots started to get out of the plane, but stiffened at the sound of a helicopter. It landed and out stepped the governor of the state of Vera Cruz. "I'm here to spend a few days relaxing on my hacienda," he said.

"Sir," the missionaries explained, "we've spent most of the day trying to get around bad weather and were forced to land since there's no visibility ahead."

"I understand," the governor replied. "Why don't you spend the night with me."

The next morning he asked one of his men to fill their tanks with aviation fuel and refused to take anything for it. "It's a pleasure," he said, "to serve men like you who are giving your lives to help the people of South America."

"Thank you so much for all your kindness."

"I got up early this morning and wrote an official letter to Mexican customs officers." He handed the letter to Clyde. "Give this to the officer at the border and you won't be delayed for a customs inspection."

Back in the air over Mexico, Clyde said, "Yesterday, Don, when I saw the six men on horses with machine guns, I wouldn't have believed we'd meet the governor and get treated so royally. God is really good."

Superb weather made for smooth flying all the way to Managua and another night of rest. The following day they reached Panama with its famous canal. After Panama, they headed across Colombia and Ecuador, then down the coast of Peru to the capital city of Lima.

The tower directed the *Fernando Stahl* to a red-carpeted VIP location near the main terminal. James Aitken, South American Division President; Don Christman, Inca Union President; Charles Case, president of the Upper Amazon Mission; a representative of the U. S. Embassy; Peruvian church employees—all were there to welcome the men and the new plane.

Eleanor and the children arrived two days later on a commercial airline. Mission administrators asked the Peters to study Spanish for three months in Lima.

Clyde went to the head office for Peru's bureau of Civil Aeronautics to license the plane and apply for his Peruvian pilot's license. "It will be at least six months before your license is ready," an official told him after they had finished all the paper work. "It may be longer."

"Six months! Did I hear you right? You mean I can't fly for six months?" Clyde looked downcast as he walked away.

Late that afternoon, he walked into the apartment where he stayed with his family at the Inca Union Mission headquarters. "I was sure God called us to Peru, but I'm beginning to doubt," he told his wife.

"What's happened?"

"The officials at Peru's Civil Aeronautics say it will be at least six months before I get my Peruvian pilot's license, and who knows how long it will take to get the plane licensed."

Clyde grew tired of constantly studying Spanish, so every few days he took a break and went to the airport to check the *Fernando Stahl*. He noticed that the salty air near the ocean and high humidity had begun to corrode the plane's aluminum shell. He purchased paint and Inca Union Mission administrators arranged for Alfredo Kalbermater, a missionary from Argentina, to help him refinish the plane.

Alfredo spoke Spanish as they worked, giving Clyde the advantage of learning more of the language in a practical situation. They cleaned the plane, sanded around every rivet, and sprayed primer, followed by several coats of white paint.

One day Clyde asked Alfredo, "Have you noticed the Peruvian who walks by here every day? He goes to a parked helicopter, starts the engine, and after a few minutes, shuts it down and leaves."

"Yes, it's really strange."

Clyde pulled off masking tape after finishing the beige trim. The fellow who ran the helicopter engine stood watching them. "I'm in a real fix," he said finally.

"What's the matter?" Clyde asked.

"Well, I just bought this helicopter, but I don't know how to fly it and I don't have a license. The only thing I know is how to start the engine."

"I'd like to help you," Clyde told the man, who he discovered was named Alfonso Diaz, "but I don't have a Peruvian pilot's license."

"Have you ever flown a helicopter?" Alfonso asked in perfect English.

"Yeah, I sure have. I have a U. S. helicopter instructor's license."

"You do! I'd like to get you to instruct me."

"I'm sorry," Clyde continued. "I just applied for my Peruvian license and I won't receive it for at least six months."

"Nonsense!" the would-be helicopter pilot responded. A wealthy owner of a Peruvian sugar plantation, he wanted to make a deal. "If I can get your license, will you teach me to fly my helicopter?"

God didn't bring me to Peru just to sit around, Clyde thought. *Maybe the Lord has a special plan.*

"I think I can arrange to help you," he replied. He knew he had to get approval from the mission, though.

Alfonso excused himself, walked to a telephone in a nearby building, and returned in a few minutes. "What are you doing this afternoon at 2:00?"

"I'll be here working on the plane," Clyde answered.

"Could you arrange to go with me to Civil Aeronautics at 2:00? I can pick you up at 1:30 so we get there on time."

"Sure, I'll be ready."

At 2:00 p.m. they walked into the main office at Peru's Civil Aeronautics. The same woman who had waited on Clyde before walked out with the officer who headed the licensing department. They grinned and asked Clyde to sign his name on the neatly typed license. Only days after hearing it would take a minimum of six months, Clyde put the Peruvian pilot's license in his billfold

Alfonso nudged him. "When do I start my helicopter instruction?"

"Let's go have the first lesson right now."

Back at the apartment that night, Clyde pulled out his billfold and showed his family his Peruvian pilot's license. "Our God works things out in ways we never dreamed possible. Now I know for sure that He wants us to work for Him here in Peru."

The mission allowed Clyde to give helicopter flight instruction, and in less then three weeks Alfonso took his check ride, passed the written examination, and qualified for his license. Alfonso Díaz would prove to be a real friend and supporter of the Adventist aviation ministry.

The *Fernando Stahl*, with it's new coat of paint, looked like a true ambassador for the Lord. Clyde completed the required language study. The mission leaders asked his family to stay in Lima while he flew the newly licensed *Fernando Stahl* across the Andes to the mission air base under construction at Yarina Cocha.

Peters checked everything to make sure the plane was ready for a flight over the Andes. "Eleanor," he said, "I've got to be really careful. No missionary's every flown a single engine plane across the Andes, and one mistake can spell disaster. I will have to climb to 18,000 feet to clear the lowest pass at Ticlio." In his excitement, he failed to check one very important thing.

Holding the controls of the *Fernando Stahl*, Clyde listened to the steady roar of the powerful engine as he gained altitude. At 14,000 feet he reached for his oxygen tube. Breathing easier, he continued to circle and climb. At 18,000 feet he turned straight out over the pass.

What a view, he thought. *I've never seen more magnificent snow capped mountains under such a blue sky.* Taller peaks towered up over 22,000 feet.

Suddenly he felt dizzy and light-headed. "Dear Lord," he prayed, "what's going on? The engine's running great, but my head—it's ready to explode."

He checked his oxygen. "Oh, no! My oxygen bottle's empty. It should have been filled, and I didn't even check it. Please help me, Lord. I double checked everything on the plane and forgot the most important thing for me. Without Your breath of life, I'll never make it."

Peters asked God to help him know what to do next. "I'm over the pass, so it would waste time and money to fly back to Lima. Help me, Lord, to sit still and breathe deeply. Please don't let me pass out at the controls of Your plane."

I know God is helping me. In a few minutes I'll start descending to lower elevation. The rugged, snowcapped peaks began to disappear and everything below turned green. The *Fernando Stahl* dropped to 12,000 feet elevation and Clyde felt like he could breathe again. "Thank you, Lord, for getting me through the oxygen crisis," he prayed.

Ahead, on the Amazon side of the Andes, lay dense jungle, home of giant jaguars, huge crocodiles, and boa constrictors that can grow as long as 40 feet. In this wild jungle, covering hundreds of thousands of square miles, live some 35 primitive Indian tribes, many with no contact with civilization. They would not hesitate to pepper the body of a stranger with poison arrows at the slightest provocation.

From 5,000 feet Clyde saw occasional clusters of thatched roof huts. *This is going to be my home,* he thought. *This is where Eleanor and my children will live. With God's help, we must work in the spirit of Elder Stahl and take the story of Jesus to every possible place.*

At 3,000 feet he saw the city of Pucallpa on the Ucayali, longest tributary of the great Amazon River. Soon he spotted Yarina Cocha and a new dirt runway. A 50- by 70-foot hanger was under construction as well as two homes, one for his family and another for Alfredo and Flora Kalbermatter, both registered nurses and assigned to serve the air base doing medical work and helping with maintenance.

Clyde buzzed the runway, circled, and landed for the very first time on July 3, 1964. The *Fernando Stahl* rolled to a stop near the new hangar. Missionaries working on the air base construction ran up to the plane. "Welcome, welcome!" everyone greeted him.

He smiled. "I'm sure glad to be here. Looks like a lot of work's been going on."

"Sorry your house isn't finished yet. But listen, there's a kerosene refrigerator where we keep a good supply of boiled water." They led Clyde to a tiny thatched hut with a dirt floor. Inside it had just enough space for a kerosene stove and refrigerator. "This is real luxury," the other missionaries laughed. "In our jungle heat you will be drinking a lot, so this is where you come to get water."

"Thank you for showing me the water," Clyde said, "but where am I going to sleep?"

"See the tent over there right on the edge of Lake Yarina Cocha. It has a good mosquito net, and with a good tent fly, we think you'll stay dry when it rains. We'll provide meals until your house is finished and you get moved in with your family."

Soon Clyde discovered that his big problem in the Amazon was not crocodiles, big snakes, or jaguars. The real enemy was insects. Tiny red chiggers fastened to his legs every time he walked through grass. The swelling and itching increased when he scratched. Millions of malaria-transmitting anopheles mosquitos, hungry for human blood, swarmed out at sunset.

CHAPTER FIVE

"MAYDAY!"

Clyde's new aviation program owed a tremendous debt to missionaries such as the Stahls, Haydens, Elicks, and Taylors who had pioneered the way into the great Amazon rain forest. Charles Case, president of the Upper Amazon Mission, flew with Peters on an orientation trip to see the various missionaries who served Indian tribes and worked to open airstrips in remote areas. At Nevati, their first stop, he met Marvin and Waloma Fehrenbach. Siegfried and Evelyn Neuendorff directed the mission station at Unini.

Everywhere Clyde landed, the locals labored with primitive tools to fell huge trees and level the ground to build or improve airstrips. "You know, Elder Case," Clyde said, "these people are amazing. They all work together, and look what they accomplish without the good tools we're used to."

While the locals hacked out a runway at Shahuaya, tiny Nilda Bautista fell from the high porch of her family's palm thatched hut. The girl's tumble from the house built high on poles for protection from flood waters resulted in a broken shoulder blade and severe head and chest injuries.

The nearest hospital, at Pucallpa, was five days by dugout canoe down the Ucayali-Amazon. The Conivo Indian parents knew their injured daughter could not survive five days in a dugout under a blazing jungle sun and long nights fighting hordes of mosquitos.

For days they had worked with other villagers clearing the airstrip. Now they labored feverishly in a desperate effort to complete the project. Each tree they fell brought new hope the mission airplane would come and land. Clyde flew over on his way to another mission outpost. *The airstrip looks good. I believe it's safe for me to land,* he told himself.

He circled and the *Fernando Stahl* touched down on the new strip. Then he flew little Nilda, who could not lasted five days traveling on the river, to a hospital in Pucallpa in just 50 minutes.

Two weeks after successful surgery and medical care, he transported the child back to Shahuaya. Seeing that the girl was well, her parents and the other villagers rejoiced. "You've already repaid us for our work of carving out a jungle runway," they said. "We want the *Fernando Stahl* to come every day."

During his first few weeks Clyde spent most of his time flying in the Nevati and Unini mission territory with occasional trips back to the base for maintenance and fuel. He hauled supplies for schools, transported teachers, and made medical flights.

A messenger arrived when he was at Nevati, announcing, "Everyone in the village of Miritiriani is dying with measles. All able-bodied Campas have fled, leaving the sick unable to care for themselves." Peters immediately flew in with antibiotics and food. Most of the people in the village survived.

At another village where the epidemic struck, he found rows of empty huts. "The only survivor is a young boy," he told the Fehrenbachs while failing to hold back tears. "Entire families are dead. With just one airplane I'll never be able to meet all the needs in this vast upper Amazon Basin."

As soon as builders at Yarina Cocha completed the house next to the hangar, Eleanor and the children arrived from Lima. Clyde showed his family their new home. "Don't you like these big screened windows?" he asked. "They'll keep out insects and give good circulation in this hot, humid climate. We don't need glass panes here in the Amazon."

"The windows are great and I like the kerosene stove and refrigerator," Eleanor replied.

"Yeah, those are the same appliances they had in a hut where I got boiled water when I first came out here. There's no electricity so we'll use candles and a Coleman lantern for light at night. I think we had better put the purchase of a generator on our priority list."

For Eleanor, being a missionary wife involved much more

than homemaking. She served as air base secretary, bookkeeper, accountant, counselor, and radio operator, monitoring Clyde's flights and receiving emergency messages. Beyond that, she helped care for patients flown in for emergency medical treatment. And finally, she served as church school teacher for their oldest daughter Shelly and later for Alan and Linda when they were ready for school.

The Peters' mission home operated like a hotel. Keeping record, they discovered that in one nine-month period they furnished beds and meals to no less than three guests a night and often 15 or 16. "I could never have done this without the help of Consuelo, a young Peruvian girl," Eleanor explained. When the mission held youth camps on the air base property, Eleanor served as cook.

"Eleanor is the real missionary," Clyde claims. "I fly out on exciting trips while she stays home and does all the work." Whenever possible, he took his family on weekend trips to mission stations where they provided special music for the services and Eleanor trained local teachers for jungle Sabbath schools.

He was gone the day a woman stopped at the base and asked for Mrs. Peters. "I'm going to the hospital," she explained. "Will you please loan me 250 soles." Eleanor got the money and handed it to her. The 250 soles took a good chunk of their small monthly paycheck.

After Clyde learned about the loan when he arrived home, he said, "You're too kind, Eleanor! If we give these people money, there will be no end to it. What will you say the next time someone asks for cash? The Lord supplies our needs, but we do have three children, and we can't be giving away money all the time."

"Clyde, I had to do it," she replied patiently. "This woman needed help."

"Alright, but I'll tell you right now, you'll never see the money again!"

Recovering from surgery, the woman returned to work. One day she knocked at the Peters' front door. When Eleanor invited her in, she smiled and counted out 250 soles. She had paid the loan in full, yet each Friday for almost a year, the grateful woman showed up at Eleanor's door with a big wash pan full of tropical fruit as a gift.

"I can't believe it," Clyde declared. "These people really

do keep their word. I think they can teach me some things about appreciation."

New groups of believers formed everywhere the locals built airstrips. Peters was at Nevati, preparing to fly home, when nurse Waloma Fehrenbach rushed out to the plane. "Clyde, a woman just came running in from Aguachine, one of our newest groups. These people, just learning about Jesus, still have lots of superstitions. The woman's been 48 hours on the trail. The witch doctor blames two girls for a man's illness and plans to kill them."

"Boy, I saw something like this in a mission film back at Union College. We can't let two innocent girls die. Aguachine has a very short strip with trees at the end, but if I fly alone with a light load of fuel, I can make it in and out again." Clyde drained excess fuel from the tanks and the *Fernando Stahl* roared off the Nevati runway.

The village looks empty, he thought as he circled low over Aguachine. *Usually when I fly over everyone runs out.* Landing, he walked through the village. Silence—no sign of life, no one in sight. *They must be hiding.* Finally he went up to a house and found it full of people. One man spoke Spanish, so Clyde asked him to translate. "I want all the people to come out of their houses," Peters said.

When they were all together, he asked, "Now which one of you is the witch doctor?"

"Oh," the people said. "The witch doctor fled with his son when he heard the airplane."

"Where are the two girls?" They led him to a thatched hut. Inside he saw two little girls who had been left there to die after the witch doctor's son had beaten them in an effort to kill them. Their bodies were black and blue and one girl had a big gash in her head where she'd been hit with a machete.

Months before, Waloma had examined an old man suffering with a severe case of worms and invited him to Nevati for treatment. The superstitious man refused. Now the parasites had affected his heart. He had consulted the witch doctor who blamed the two small girls for the illness.

Clyde faced the superstitious Campas. "Please understand! These girls have nothing to do with the sick man's problems." He waited for the translation to finish.

"I want to take them to Nevati, but with the condition of

your airstrip I will never make it out of here with more weight in the plane. Please care for these girls and don't let the witch doctor harm them again. Tell him I'll be flying over to check up on him."

Three weeks later word reached Nevati that the witch doctor had sneaked back and killed one of the girls. Clyde flew straight to Aguachine. Again the village appeared empty as everyone hid in their huts. Ashamed at what had happened, they confirmed that one girl was dead. He discovered the other girl injured and alone in a hut with the door tied shut.

"The rains have stopped," he told the villagers. "Your runway is in better condition so I'm taking this girl to Nevati for treatment."

"Tribal superstitions are so deep rooted," Peters explained to the Fehrenbachs as he helped the injured girl into the clinic. "Only the Word of God can change these peoples' hearts. I'm thankful for missionaries like you who are starting mission schools where natives can learn to read and study the Bible for themselves. The Word of God will transform their lives."

Clyde was back at the air base when Julian, an inspector from Peru's Civil Aeronautics Office in Lima, showed up late one afternoon. The license for operating the *Fernando Stahl* was due to expire soon and the government had sent him to find reasons why it should not be renewed. The Peters invited him to stay in their home.

Early the next morning, Eleanor fixed breakfast in the kitchen. Julian was just getting up and Clyde worked on the airplane in the hangar. Mrs. Peters, who monitored the radio, started shouting, "Clyde, there's an emergency in Puerto Putaya"

Her husband flipped on the transmitter. "Our plane will leave immediately!" he broadcast.

Julian came out. "Sorry, there's no breakfast yet," Clyde said. "I've got to make an emergency flight to Puerto Putaya. Why don't you come along."

Reaching their destination, they found that someone had shot a village leader at close range with a shotgun. Julian nearly fainted when he saw blood gushing from a wound where the gunshot had blown off part of the man's abdomen, leaving a hole the size of a hand. They loaded the dying man in the plane and rushed him to the Pucallpa Hospital where immediate surgery saved his life.

At a late breakfast that morning, Julian looked across the table at Clyde. "Politicians back in Lima have no business trying to shut down an air program like this. I'll do everything I can to make sure your aviation mission continues."

Julian, however, faced pressure from officials who insisted that he fly the *Fernando Stahl* to Lima for inspection. The Peruvian Civil Aeronautics Agency told Clyde that "Julian has been praising your work in the jungle. We're renewing the license to operate your plane. Please forgive us for making you bring it all the way to Lima."

His flawless flight over the Andes gave Clyde hope for a good journey back to the Amazon base. Although the Helio Courier is an ideal airplane for the jungle, it's a poor performer in high altitudes.

After he climbed up through coastal fog he saw a thick layer of clouds covering the Andes. *I really should go back to Lima, but our budget is so tight. I hate to put extra time on the engine and it'll save money if I fly on over the Andes now. I'll climb on up through the clouds and take a look.*

At 18,000 feet, Clyde trimmed the engine, sat back, and listened to the steady whir of the motor. The sea of clouds ahead looked as smooth as glass. Mountain peaks stuck out above the clouds and he knew the exact location of Ticlio Pass. *The engine's running fine.* He relaxed. *In about 50 miles, I'll be over the worst of this.*

Then without warning the engine started missing. *Oh no!* Clyde worked the controls. *I never should have tried this. I can turn back, but I'm sure I've already crossed the pass. If I turn around, I'll be flying into the most dangerous part of the mountains.*

Immediately the plane began losing altitude. Clyde tried to smooth out the rough engine but it only grew worse and he rapidly lost altitude. "Dear Lord," he prayed, "if this is my day, I'm ready, but this is Your airplane. If it's Your will, please save the mission plane."

The *Fernando Stahl* dipped into the clouds and Clyde flew on instruments. Desperately, he tried to hold a heading on the nearest airport at San Ramon. *At the rate I'm losing altitude, I'll never make it!*

Switching on the radio, he grabbed the mike. "Mayday! Mayday!" he shouted into it. "I just crossed Ticlio. The engine's acting up. My plane's coming down!"

Again and again he radioed, "I'm going to crash in the mountains!" Besides losing altitude, the wings started icing up. More fear gripped him when the air inlet froze over, causing the airspeed indicator to stop working. *I can't fly on instruments inside a cloud without knowing the airspeed.*

The plane kept dropping. As he prayed again he broke out at the bottom of a cloud. Mountains surrounded him, a quarter of a mile this way, an eighth of a mile the other way, only a few hundred feet in another direction. He had dropped 2,000 feet.

"Thank You, Lord! The engine's running fine now." The highest pass behind him, he sneaked under the clouds and around mountain peaks all the way to Nevati.

After landing, Clyde walked straight to the mission clinic, found a bed, and flopped down. Elder Fehrenbach came in and asked, "What's the matter? You're terribly pale."

"Well, Marvin, I've just had a real rough flight."

"Sorry! Tell me about it."

"I should have flown back to Lima," Clyde said, "but I came on even though clouds covered the Andes. You can't imagine what it's like to be up there all by yourself when the engine starts missing and the plane begins to lose altitude."

"But you had the Lord with you!"

"You're right. I asked God to save the plane. Here I was coming down inside a cloud, ice formed on the wings, and the airspeed indicator froze up. I expected to crash any second. Now I'm completely drained, but thank the Lord—He watched over the *Fernando Stahl* and saved my life."

CHAPTER SIX

"KAMETZA!"

The Fehrenbachs worked at Nevati on the Pachitea River. The Neuendorffs operated the Unini Mission Station just off the Ucayali River. Between the two rivers lay a range of mountains known as the Gran Pajonal, considered one of the wildest areas in the entire upper Amazon jungle.

Mission president Charles Case sent letters encouraging missionaries to enter new areas and build airstrips wherever possible. Siegfried Neuendorff prayed about the possibility of taking the gospel into the dangerous Gran Pajonal. He left his wife, Evelyn, in charge of the mission station, planning to return in three or four days.

With two Campa Indians he began to climb a range of mountains to reach the Gran Pajonal. At the end of the fourth day they reached a village clearing. The place seemed abandoned. When the Campa guide whistled, Indians, armed with bows and arrows, leaped out of the trees like monkeys. Instantly, men and women with faces painted a brilliant red surrounded Siegfried and his Campa companions.

Fear rules this vast area—fear of revenge, fear of the spirits, fear of the witch doctor, fear of strangers. Fearful Indians climbed trees when they heard the missionary coming. Now, they stood and stared, awed at the sight of a six-foot-four-inch *gringo*. Compared to them, he was a giant. Finally, they began to make their way slowly back to their huts.

Chief Huánaco, who had killed several men, motioned for the visitors to follow him to a hut where he lived with several wives. They served a supper of boiled *yuca*—a stringy white root eaten like potatoes—as well as roasted corn, pineapple, and sweet potatoes. After dark, the Campa interpreter helped missionary Neuendorff conduct the first Christian meeting the people had ever attended.

The next morning, while eating more boiled *yuca* for breakfast, Siegfried watched women sitting on the ground eating maggots. *Not the dessert I want*, he thought.

After breakfast, he held another meeting. The people responded with enthusiasm and Siegfried questioned Chief Huánaco. "How would you like to have a teacher come to instruct you more about God and heaven? How would you like to have your boys and girls learn to read and write?"

Chief Huánaco grunted, "*Kametza*—yes, send us a teacher." Siegfried promised to return and then followed his Campa guides out of the village back to Unini where his wife waited and worried.

Evelyn had expected her husband home in three or four days. He had already been gone five. Before arriving home, he would experience encounters with poisonous snakes while walking barefoot, lack food and water, lose 15 pounds—and after getting lost, end up at Nevati instead of Unini

Clyde rescued him and flew back to Unini on the fifteenth day. His wife and daughter could hardly believe it when he announced, "I'm going back to the Gran Pajonal. I promised Chief Huánaco that if they build an airstrip, we'll bring them a teacher."

Rufino Valles and his wife Elsa volunteered to serve as teachers. Two days later, Clyde brought three axes and five machetes to use in clearing a new airstrip. "Let me fly you to Oventeni," he offered. "This will save a lot of walking. You should be able to hike in from there with all your equipment in one day."

"Wonderful!" Siegfried exclaimed. Telling his family goodbye, he climbed into the *Fernando Stahl* along with the teacher and his wife. In minutes, they flew what had taken Siegfried three days of walking. After they landed, Siegfried, with the Indian teacher Rufino and his wife Elsa, started the long trek to find Chief Huánaco.

Chief for the whole area, Huánaco led them to Tsioventeni. After everyone in the village came together, Neuendorff explained, "I've brought you a teacher. Your children will learn to read the Word of God. But before anything else, we want to build an airstrip so our mission plane can land."

Then he continued, "I have an urgent request. We want you to stop making alcoholic beverages. Please promise you won't drink *mazato* any more. Stop having *fiestas* where you drink and dance all night. We want you to be happy and to live for Jesus."

"Kametza," Huánaco grunted. "We will do as you request."

Over 200 huge trees needed to be cut down and the ground leveled. After five days, Clyde flew over to make sure Siegfried Neuendorff had reached his destination. He saw the people working on the airstrip and picked up the microphone to call the air base. "Wish you could see the whole village out here working together. Siegfried really inspires the locals."

The Campas worked from sunrise to sunset. In the evenings, Siegfried held meetings to share the story of Jesus who was preparing a home in heaven for His people. When Friday came, he explained, "There will be no work on the seventh-day. We will rest and worship our Creator."

Work stopped early on Friday afternoon so everyone could clean their houses, take baths, and be ready for the Sabbath. Siegfried and Rufino worked together to teach the people the joy of honoring Jesus on His holy day.

Clyde flew in and out of Nevati, helping the Fehrenbach's take vaccine to remote areas since smallpox and measles had wiped out whole villages. One evening he talked with Marvin. "I think we can complete this vaccination project by noon tomorrow. Then I'd like to fly to Tsioventeni. Siegfried should have the airstrip ready and I can pick him up."

In the morning, Marvin, Waloma, and their son, Rick, flew with Clyde and completed vaccinating the people in the two remaining villages. Finished, they flew back to Nevati. The propeller had barely stopped turning when Clyde asked, "Waloma, you're all dressed up in your nurses' uniform. How would you like to go to Tsioventeni? You could vaccinate the people there too."

"Sure," she answered without hesitation. "I've been hoping for a chance to visit Tsioventeni and the Gran Pajonal."

"There's one problem," though. "I don't want to break up families, but I think we better leave Marvin here. I flew over Tsioventeni yesterday. We won't have any trouble getting in, but a couple stumps still remain at one end of the runway, and

I don't want too much weight when I take off the first time on this new strip."

Marvin chuckled. "Go ahead Clyde, take Waloma. She can care for any medical needs. You should be back in two hours and that won't delay my dinner too much. I'll be going there soon anyway," he added, "but this might be the only chance for Waloma to visit these people."

They flew over deep canyons, rugged mountains, and gorgeous waterfalls few people had ever seen. "It's only a short time since Siegfried walked through this wild area," Waloma remarked. If she had known what faced her, she would have insisted that Clyde do a 180° turn and fly straight back to Nevati.

He buzzed the new strip while Siegfried motioned frantically for the plane to land. The damp soil made braking unnecessary. "How will this soft ground affect our takeoff?" Waloma asked. But the excitement of watching a remote tribe see the mission plane land for the first time quickly erased the idea of any problem from her consciousness.

Indians, faces painted red, surrounded the plane. The men's hair reached their shoulders. Both men and women showed the tribal insignia—a perforated lower lip. Many had a 45-caliber shell protruding from the hole. They had picked up the shells after hunters passed through their jungle area. In the past they had adorned themselves with a piece of bone through their lower lip.

Clyde unloaded provisions for the teacher and his wife. "I'm sure glad you landed," Siegfried said. "I've been living and working with these people for seven days. As soon as you and Waloma finish the vaccinations, I want you to fly me to Unini."

Waloma spotted a big fire. "What are they doing? Burning brush from the runway?"

"No, they're burning the brewery," Siegfried responded. "They promised not to make *mazato* any more. Now they're burning the canoe-like vat used for making alcoholic drinks. Everyone used to sit around, chew *yuca*, spit it in the vat, add water, and then leave it to ferment."

"Then what?" Waloma wanted to know.

"They'd have a *fiesta* and everyone got dead drunk. I'm amazed how fast the gospel changes these people," Siegfried continued. "The teacher's been here only a few days and it's a totally different village from what I saw just a few weeks ago.

They've even stopped eating wild pigs."

The tall missionary had no trouble persuading the people to let the white uniformed nurse vaccinate them. When she finished, Clyde said, "Let's get going. I'm glad Siegfried walked in without a lot of baggage. We don't need any extra weight."

They boarded the *Fernando Stahl* and Clyde prayed for a safe trip. "Wait," he said. "We've prayed, but I'm not comfortable with the soft strip. We're at 4,600 feet elevation. Most of the short runways where I take off are less than 1,000 feet above sea level."

"Does this mean I have to get out?" Siegfried asked.

"I think both of you better get out. Let me do a trial take-off." The plane minus its two passengers barely lifted over the two stumps at the end of the short runway.

Returning, Clyde organized everyone into stompers, rollers, and choppers. Women and children used bare feet or small logs to pack the soft earth. Men chopped out the remaining stumps. They cut a huge log so they could roll the plane back further, adding more distance to the runway.

After two hours Peters said, "I think we've done everything we can do today. I'll make another test flight. Perhaps the next time we can go together—or at least I'll take Waloma and come back for Siegfried later."

After the second try, Clyde said, "We'd better remove some of the fuel." The teacher brought two five-gallon cans and the Indians contributed large gourds that they used for water. Attempting to lighten the plane, they siphoned out as much gasoline as possible. Clyde lifted off the dirt runway, circled, and returned, shaking his head.

"You don't need to say it, Clyde." Waloma spoke. "I'm not getting in that plane. Let's find another solution."

"The only solution is for you and Siegfried to walk to Oventeni."

Siegfried had followed that trail several times. "It'll take seven hours," he said. "It won't be a problem for me, but Waloma? Isn't there some other way to get her out of here?"

"The only way is to make the runway longer. The Indians have promised to do that, but it will take several days," Clyde, in the pilot's seat, leaned out the window. "I'll fly to Nevati and let Marvin know what happened. Then I'll see you about 10:00 tomorrow morning at Oventeni."

Waloma stood watching the plane wave its wings and disappear on the way to tell her husband about the predicament. "Look at me," she mused. "I'm still in my nurse's uniform—and walk all night? I didn't even bring shoes. All I have are these thongs I'm wearing."

Siegfried laughed. "It's only been a few weeks since I walked out of here barefoot, and I thought I would die."

Waloma tried to borrow clothing from Elsa, the teacher's wife, but everything was too small. She changed into a *cushma* loaned to her by Rufino and put her uniform in a plastic bag. Elsa provided *yuca* and pineapple for the trip, they prayed, and the three—Siegfried, Waloma, and a Campa named Juan— started down the trail.

"Oventeni! Oventeni! We're going to Oventeni?" The thought pierced Waloma's mind like a dagger. "That's where a commercial pilot found a body filled with arrows like pins in a pincushion!"

"Don't worry," Siegfried spoke with confidence. "With our Campa guide, we won't have any problem. Perhaps we can spend the night at an Indian village."

In less than two hours the sun had dropped below the horizon. The equator lacks twilight, and when the sun sets it gets dark almost immediately. Juan stopped abruptly as they came to a jungle clearing. They could hear the slow, steady beat of drums and wild shouts of dancing Indians. "Fiesta! Masato!" Juan muttered. "They make me drink. I no drink more. You go on. I go back."

"No, no!" Siegfried pleaded. "Please, stay with us! Isn't there a way for us to walk around the village?"

"No," Juan insisted. He tossed the small bundle he carried into Siegfried's hands, stepped back into the jungle, and disappeared.

"What shall we do now?" Siegfried asked. "I'm glad Juan is determined not to drink, but I didn't think he would leave us like this."

"Let's keep going," Waloma replied. "The Indians may be too drunk to even notice us. With the noise of their drums, they won't hear us."

Without a flashlight, they walked on in the darkness, sometimes stumbling and falling. Carefully they crept through tall pampa grass and around the Campa settlement. "Angels have watched over us so far," Siegfried said as they walked on the dark trail beyond the village. "The Lord will see us through the night."

Arriving at a clearing, the dark trail disappeared in tall grass. "We can't afford to get lost and miss the plane. We better spend the night here," he suggested. They stepped back under a clump of trees, "I have one air mattress, one blanket, and a mosquito net. You can use my equipment, Waloma."

"Siegfried, you're tall and thin. You need the air mattress and my *cushma* will keep me warm so I don't need a blanket."

"OK," he agreed, "but you take the mosquito net." He blew up his air mattress and pulled the blanket over his long body.

Waloma moved away a modest distance and curled up in the borrowed *cushma*. "I'm sure grateful for the use of your mosquito net, Siegfried," she called. The monotonous beat of jungle drums echoed in the distance. Waloma held up the mosquito net each time a vampire bat dived near her face. Every bone in her body ached, and she longed for morning.

The haunting sounds of the jungle vanished in the roaring echoes of thunder followed by bursts of blinding lighting. Dawn brought a torrential downpour. Siegfried quickly stuffed everything he carried, except food, into a rubberized bag. Then he and Waloma sat back to back on the bag holding the air mattress over their heads with a blanket draped over it to form a tent as protection from the heavy rain.

Half an hour later, the deluge slowed to a steady rain. "We've got to get going if we're going to meet Clyde," Siegfried said. They tried to walk with the makeshift tent over them, but finally gave up, wrung out the blanket, and stuffed it into Siegfried's bag along with the air mattress.

After slipping in the mud and falling repeatedly, Waloma threw away her troublesome thongs. With bare feet, her toes pressed into the mud on the trail, she slipped less often. At 10:00 a.m. they heard the *Fernando Stahl* fly over and land at Oventeni. "I wish we were there," Waloma exclaimed.

"Me too," Siegfried replied. "We've still got a lot of miles to go."

An hour went by and the plane took off. "Is Clyde going to fly away and leave us?" Waloma asked.

"I think he's flying low looking for us." Siegfried stepped into a clearing, pulled off his shirt, and waved it to catch Clyde's attention. The plane circled low, dipped a wing in recognition, and returned to Oventeni to wait.

Falling again, Waloma felt sharp pains in her knee. "I'm not keeping up with you Siegfried," she called. "I've just got to stop and rest. I wish Clyde had a helicopter."

At the plane where Clyde waited, curious children spilled out of the jungle. He took out his trumpet and taught them Christian songs.

With aching bones, a sore knee, and exhausted from a sleepless night, Waloma limped toward the Oventeni runway. Spotting the *Fernando Stahl* and Clyde Peters, Waloma exclaimed, "This is the most beautiful sight I've seen."

Still limping, Waloma at last reached the plane. "Clyde, God has used you and the mission plane to save many lives. Now it's going to save mine." She backed into the plane and sat on the floor behind the seats.

Siegfried and Waloma had spent nine hours walking and a sleepless night to reach Oventeni. Within minutes Clyde had them back over Tsioventeni, waving to people Waloma had met the day before. They touched down at San Pablo to pick up Marvin. Angry thoughts filled the husband's mind when He saw an Indian wearing a *cushma* sitting in the back of the plane. *Why did Clyde bring some Indian and not my wife?* Then he caught himself. *Indians are important, too, and I shouldn't feel this way.*

He turned to Clyde. "Where's Waloma?"

"Don't you know your own wife?"

Marvin looked again and laughed, then climbed in beside her. "What are you doing in a man's *cushma*? You're covered with mud, and I've never seen your hair in such a mess."

"Without a comb, I couldn't do anything with my hair, and there was no place on the Oventeni runway to wash up."

Clyde dropped the Fehrenbachs off at Nevati and flew on to Unini with Siegfried.

During her short visit at Tsioventeni, Waloma had called Clyde's attention to Marivanchi, wife of the village chief, who had a terrible ulcerated fungus infection on her leg. Before he left Nevati, Waloma said, "Clyde, I think I have medication that can cure this woman's leg." She gave him the special ointment with instructions that he treat Marivanchi at the first opportunity.

On his next flight to the Gran Pajonal, Clyde took two nurses with him. Seven weeks had passed since wild Indians had surprised Siegfried by leaping out of the trees and surrounding him. Marivanchi showed complete trust in the missionary nurses as they cleaned the ugly oozing mess on her leg and applied the medication. They left a supply of the ointment with the teacher to continue the treatment.

When Clyde returned a few weeks later, Marivanchi sat on a log, pointing to her leg. "*Kametza!*"she said in Campa. All infection gone, the skin on her leg was clear and smooth. *Kametza,* a Campa word, meant wonderful, good, or even beautiful.

It's *Kametza* when people learn about Jesus and change the way they live. Missionaries marveled at the transformation in Tsioventeni. No one drank, their ornaments disappeared, and the gun shells came out of the lower lips. The people washed the bright red paint from their faces and stopped killing people with their bows and arrows.

About a year later Marivanchi became one of the first from Tsio venteni to give her heart to Jesus and accept baptism. Her husband, Sha wingo, chief of Tsioventeni, had used his bow and arrows to kill at least four people. He wanted to be baptized too, but chose to wait and make some things right first.

CHAPTER SEVEN

PISTACOS AND RIFLE GREASE

Flying over the Gran Pajonal, Clyde could see dozens of small Campa compounds, usually four or five huts grouped together where the Indians slept on palm leaf mats on dirt floors. Each village had its witch doctor who exerted a strong hold on the people.

One witch doctor, fearing he might lose power over his people, started a rumor. "Don't have anything to do with the airplane that flies overhead. Don't ever go to Nevati for medical treatment. If you do go, *pistacos* will get you. They will put you in a big pot and boil you down until only grease is left. Foreigners will use this grease to lubricate their rifles and shotguns."

Superstitious Indians believed his tale and it kept many from using the medical service provided at Nevati.

Quinchiquiri, a Campa boy about 12 years old, helped his father fell trees in the rain forest. One day a tree fell on the boy, a limb piercing his lung and pinning him to the ground. His father raced back to the village, got a few men along with the boy's mother, and working together, they lifted the tree off the boy. The horrified mother gasped at the sight of a piece of the broken limb protruding from the huge hole in her son's back. Blood spurted from the wound, but they saw no sign of breathing.

"Quinchiquiri's dead!" the mother screamed. As they carried him out, he started breathing. The superstitious parents faced a dilemma. Should they take their bleeding son to the witch doctor only a few hundred yards away, or should they carry the boy for three days and nights over a rugged trail to

56

reach Nevati and Christian medical help?

They had watched the witch doctor mix tobacco juice and alcohol and pray to the spirits, but they didn't see how it could heal a serious injury. Although they had heard of miracles happening at Nevati, they still feared *pistacos* might cook their boy until only grease remained. But the Holy Spirit worked on their Campa hearts, and the parents collected their son, some Indian friends, and headed down the trail toward Nevati. Three days later the missionaries examined the boy and realized the case was more than they could handle. They made an emergency radio call to the mission air base in Pucallpa. Clyde hurried to the hangar, fueled the plane, and an hour later, landed at the Nevati Mission Station.

Cringing at the sight of a body covered with blood and filth, he asked, "You want me to fly this youngster to Pucallpa?"

The wound in the boy's back was full of maggots and a piece of broken branch still lodged there. He wore a dirty cushma and his body smelled like that of a dead animal. The edges of the inside of his eyelids should have been bright pink. Instead, they were almost white. The Indian boy had lost a great deal of blood.

Feeling sick in his stomach, Clyde helped carry the boy to the plane and laid him on the floor behind the pilot's seat. Juan Ucayali, a Campa translator, explained to Quinchiquiri that they would take him to the hospital. "When you start feeling better, don't run off to the jungle. Just stay there and they will bring you back to your parents."

Before starting the airplane engine, Clyde asked Juan Ucayali to pray. Clyde noticed the boy's mother standing behind her husband. Campa spouses seldom stand together and never put their arms around each other in public. The woman was crying. She had seen the *Fernando Stahl* fly over, but she'd never been close to an airplane before.

It made the witch doctor's stories seemed all the more plausible. *They haven't made my boy well at all, but they're putting him in this device. Then they will take him away and cook him down to nothing but grease. The witch doctor's right—I'll never see my son again.*

Clyde tapped the little fellow on the shoulder and smiled. "Hey, you little rascal, why don't you smile? Come on, be nice. I'm being nice to you."

Look at this little guy—he's almost like a little animal. Questions filled Clyde's mind. *Is it really worth all we're doing to try to save him?*

As he closed the airplane door he glanced at the parents. Their fearful faces were painted red like all the Indians from the Gran Pajonal. The father wore a long bunch of bright bird feathers hanging down his back. Clyde started the engine and taxied out for takeoff. When he applied power, the little fellow grabbed his leg in a death grip and didn't let go all the way to Pucallpa. Throughout the journey he lay on the floor, shaking and holding Clyde's leg.

How can I ever get to a little guy like this? He wondered. *How can we teach him anything? Can his parents ever understand what God's love is all about?*

Landing at the base, he taxied to the hanger, cut the engine, and coasted in. When Clyde opened the door, there stood his youngest child, 4-year-old Linda. *Oh no!* he thought. *Our Linda! She seems to have the ability to play with the dirtiest children. They can be absolutely filthy, yet she goes out and plays with them, and everyone has a great time.*

Glancing into the plane, the child smiled, "Hola, ¿Como estás?" She didn't know the Campa boy couldn't understand Spanish. But Quinchiquiri looked at her and smiled too.

Clyde watched them. *Amazing! This little guy does know how to smile.* The boy looked a mess—his body odor made everyone want to hold their nose—but Linda thought he was great. Clyde loaded Quinchiquiri into a jeep and headed for the hospital.

The doctor checked the young patient and shook his head, "I don't know how this boy is alive. You say they carried him on a trail for three days?"

Peters looked straight at the doctor. "Please do all you can to keep him alive. It would be wonderful if God would heal him and we could take him back to his parents."

The doctor ordered a blood transfusion, pulled the stick out of the lung, and scraped maggots from the hole in the boy's back. Quinchiquiri felt better immediately.

"Anything you can think of that would be impossible to live through, he already has," the doctor said. "And he's still awake and alert. We can't sew up the wound. It's been open too long and will have to heal on its own."

"Won't he die with the hole in his back?" Clyde asked.

"The best we can do is pray he won't. We'll give him a lot of antibiotics. And he's full of worms and will need medication to take care of that too. I think he'll be better off if you just take him home and care for him. We'll send medicines with you."

The mission pilot took the youngster back to the base. "Eleanor, they won't keep this boy at the hospital. Will you make a bed for him in the hangar?"

"We can't do that," she said. "We don't speak Campa, and we need to keep him here in our house where we can watch him."

"OK, if its got to be that way."

The Peters didn't own many good sheets, but Eleanor got out a couple of their best and put them on a bed for the young patient. "This little guy doesn't know the difference between a sheet and a blanket," her husband interrupted. "He's never seen a sheet. Dear, do we have to use those good sheets for him?"

"Yes! Although we can't talk to him, we can treat him like a king. We can treat him the way Jesus treats us."

Listening to Eleanor, Clyde felt ashamed. "I'm amazed the Lord doesn't strike me dead. I want to leave him in the hangar, but you bring him in the house, give him the best sheets, and I know you will give him the best food too."

The children watched their mother make the bed for their new friend. Shelly and Alan thought it was great—Linda thought it was wonderful. Quinchiquiri just smiled. They had cleaned him up a little at the hospital, but he still needed a bath. The Peters helped him bathe without getting any water into the wound in his back. Then Clyde showed him how to use the bathroom, because they had one of those fancy toilets you have to flush.

The boy ate the food Eleanor prepared. She brought him orange juice with ice cubes. He howled when his tongue touched the ice, having never seen ice before. And he had never seen a kerosene stove—not even an old fashioned one with wicks. When Eleanor lit a match, Quinchiquiri watched the blue flame go all the way around the wick burner. She put on a pan of water and in a short time it started to boil. Quinchiquiri must have thought, *What would my mom do with one of these?*

At worship time that evening, Clyde peeked during prayer. They had all knelt around the bed in the living room. Quinchiquiri climbed out and knelt down by the three Peters children. Their father watched how when they folded their hands, he held his the same way. When they closed their eyes, he shut his too.

Clyde felt a tear on his cheek. *Do missions pay? Can Jesus save primitive people? I think the Lord is trying to humble me for the way*

I've been thinking. After prayer he commented, "If this boy's parents lived in the United States, they would qualify for Ph.D. degrees in jungle survival."

At breakfast Eleanor served gravy on toast and Quinchiquiri loved it. Then they gave him bananas, papaya, and other things he was used to at his home back in the forest. Clyde took him back to the bathroom to be sure he knew how to use all the equipment.

At home the boy went to a spring and carried water in a clay pot. Now he learned how to turn a faucet and watch water fill a bathroom sink. Clyde gave him a comb and a mirror and showed him how to wash his face and comb his hair. After that he'd go in there and comb his hair many times a day.

The youngster stayed in the Peter's home for 30 days. As he got better, he played outside with the children. Although he came from the heart of some of Peru's wildest jungle, yet he acted like a perfect little gentleman. He loved Eleanor's cooking and she liked to cook for him.

Because of the language barrier, Clyde asked a Campa teacher, spending a day at the base, to talk to the boy. "You're about well now," the teacher explained. "The mission pilot is going to take you in the airplane and fly you back to your parents." Suddenly Quinchiquiri's ear-to-ear smile vanished.

Oh, Oh! Clyde thought. *This little guy wants to stay here the rest of his life. I'm not sure we can handle that.*

In less than an hour the child had disappeared. "We can't let anything happen to him now," Clyde worried. "He's well and needs to return to his village. I'm responsible to get him back to his parents." Everybody at the base and the locals living around the area searched for the boy, but no one could find him.

"Lord, You know where the boy is," the Peters family prayed. "Please bring him back."

An hour later, Clyde glanced down the runway and saw Quinchiquiri walking out of the jungle holding something in his hands. When the boy came closer, Clyde saw that the sling Quinchiquiri had worn around his neck when he had arrived at the air base was still there. But now he had a big smile—bigger than any until then.

"Boy, am I glad to see you!" Clyde said. "What do you have in your hands anyway? Are you trying to work on us so you can stay a little longer?"

Clyde imagined all kinds of things as Quinchiquiri motioned

for them to come over to the bird cage. The Peters' children understood and opened its door. The boy reached in and let go of something. It was the most beautiful little bird they'd ever seen. Peruvians called it *siete colores*, a seven-colored tanager.

The boy knew he was leaving and wanted to do something special for Shelly, Alan, and Linda. He had taken his slingshot and walked around for several hours, getting himself all scratched up. Having made a soft ball of mud, he used it in his slingshot to knock the bird out of the air without injuring it.

"If I tried to do this," Clyde told his family, "I'd still be making mud balls. This boy caught the bird without breaking a bone in its body and gave it to us as a gift of gratitude. He has a heart of gold. Wouldn't you like to spend eternity with someone like him?"

For his flight home, the boy wore his *cushma* and sling and carried the comb and mirror. The Peters gave him a few clothes. Although he really didn't have much, he was happy. For a month he had watched people come and go in the airplane. Now he climbed up in the seat and fastened the seat belt as if he'd done it a hundred times. The aircraft taxied to the end of the runway and turned around for takeoff. Clyde revved up the engine wondering, *Is this little fellow going to get scared?*

The boy's face broke out in a big contented smile. He kept looking out, and as they flew up the Pachitea River, he could see dozens of dugout canoes. He patted the airplane. "*Kametza!*" Before long the *Fernando Stahl* touched down at Nevati, and Clyde killed the engine. As the plane rolled to a stop, he could see Quinchiquiri's parents. People tried to hold them back, but they broke away and ran to the plane.

Quinchiquiri jumped out, joining his parents. The next 20 minutes turned into one big blur of Campa. Clyde didn't understand much that anyone said, but he kept hearing such words as Señora, Alan, Shelly, Linda, and *Capitán*. He knew the boy was talking about him and his family. Also he assumed that Quinchiquiri must have told them about the ice cubes, the white sheets, and even the toast and gravy, plus how the Peters had worship and talked to Jesus every day in their home.

The Campa mother kept wiping away tears—tears of joy. The missionaries had not boiled her son to a chunk of rifle grease. He was alive and well. She pushed up his cushma and rubbed her hand across the scar on his back. The hole into his lung had completely healed over.

"The witch doctor's story about *pistacos* can't be true," she told Juan Ucayali. At Nevati she and her husband learned there is a God in heaven who loves Campas and works with the hands of medical professionals to heal human bodies.

Clyde stepped into the mission station office for a few minutes. Returning, he saw a huge pile of *yuca* under the airplane wing. Quinchiquiri's parents had made some kind of a deal with other Campas at Nevati. Juan Ucayali explained. "This is a gift from them to show appreciation for what's been done for their son. It's for you, your wife, Shelly, Alan, and especially Linda."

Clyde stared at it with his mouth open. "Tell this family there's enough *yuca* to fill three planes like the *Fernando Stahl*. I'll take what I can. The boy lived in our home for 30 days. I didn't like the idea but now I see, I'm the one who's receiving the greatest blessing."

On the flight back to the base he reviewed it all. *My wife and children didn't hesitate to give him their best. When I think of Quinchiquiri, I will always remember that often the people we least expect are some of the best candidates for the kingdom of heaven.*

"Dear God," he prayed, "help me to be kind and always show love and respect for all your children."

After servicing the plane, Clyde flew to Tsioventeni for the first time in weeks. He found the school closed. The new teacher, a young Campa named Melita and trained at Unini, had been in bed for several days, having fallen after school one day. Now her foot and ankle were swollen, causing severe pain. Clyde contacted Siegfried by radio and explained the situation. The men decided to fly her out to Pucallpa.

An x-ray revealed a broken bone just above her ankle so they put on a cast. The young woman stayed in the Peter's home. Two weeks later the doctor released Melita and Clyde flew her back to Tsioventeni.

He knew that a whooping cough epidemic had raged in nearby Pauti. Rufino and his wife had transferred there to start a new school. *I better fly over and see how he is getting along.* A huge thunder head rose into the sky ahead. Clyde descended toward Pauti just as torrential rain broke loose. *I can't land in this. The strip here is marginal at best.* He circled a couple of times and flew on toward Unini. He listened to the noise of the engine and pelting rain. Then almost as if he heard a voice in the cockpit, the words came to him, "Clyde, go back to Pauti!"

"Are you talking to me, Lord?" The impression became so strong that he banked the plane and headed back. The heavy rains let up a little. Carefully he guided the plane down under the clouds onto the muddy airstrip. Water still poured off the palm thatched huts as he landed.

Rufino, out of breath, raced to the aircraft. "Clyde, for three days we've been praying for the plane to come. My wife's sick and I'm afraid my children will die."

"I'm sorry," Peters responded as he listened.

"Many people in this village are ill. We heard the plane coming, and when it flew away, our hopes of getting medical attention vanished. Then we all knelt down and prayed. We were still on our knees when we heard the plane returning. God sent you back!"

Their answer to prayer made a tremendous impression on the group of new believers who were just learning about Jesus and His love. Clyde used up all his medicine treating patients who suffered severe respiratory complications from whooping cough. Afterward he flew out and returned with more medication. At the base that evening he told Eleanor, "God asked me to land in Pauti today. He's definitely guiding our aviation ministry."

Often Clyde stopped at Puerto Yarina on the Pachitea River. Each time he made the final approach, he saw a huge crocodile sunning on a sandbar. "Why don't we do something about this crocodile?" he kept asking the people.

But the villagers would laugh. "Don't worry, he doesn't bother anybody." They regarded the situation as humorous.

One day Clyde arrived and said, "Let's go out there and kill that crocodile."

The people grinned. "We don't think you can."

"Come on," he urged, "I'll show you how to hunt crocodiles." He pulled out a pistol and indicated how it held six powerful shells. "This is a real crocodile machine. It'll get the crocodile every time. Come with me. Let's go."

The villagers laughed, but they were polite and respectful. "All right, *Captián* Peters, what do you want us to do?"

"First, we've got to sneak out on that island." It meant that they would have to keep very low and go through mud and shallow water. The men got down on their bellies and followed Clyde across almost 1,000 feet of muck and mud. When they reached the sandy beach they still had to crawl since the area was almost flat. Clyde tried to keep sand out of the gun.

"If we stand up, it's the end of the hunt," he explained. Reaching a little rise, they peeked over and saw the big reptile still quite a way off. After backing off on their bellies, they crept closer to where the crocodile rested in the sun.

I really don't know what I'm doing, Clyde had to admit to himself. "Listen," he cautioned the natives, "I'm the only one with a gun. Your machetes will be worthless if the crocodile decides to attack."

The Indians crawled alongside him and whispered, "Look, he's right beyond this rise." Not more than 50 feet away, the huge reptile lay there like a big old log, its eyes sticking up out of his head. As Clyde stared into them, the crocodile saw him. "I've got to do something quick," he whispered, "but I can't shoot from this position." He sat up and aimed.

Splash! Before Clyde could pull the trigger the crocodile hit the water and disappeared. *I brought these men here.* Clyde fired several shots. *The least I can do is give them a thrill by making a lot of noise.* The Indians laughed.

"Guess you can see," Clyde also laughed, "that I'm no crocodile hunter."

Covered with mud, they marched back to the village. Clyde placed the Magnum 357 under the seat of the plane and headed for the river to clean up. While washing, he watched the men scrubbing their *cushmas. Back in the civilized world, they wouldn't stand for my foolishness. But these men are so patient and polite.*

The villagers acted pleased for the adventure. "*Capitán,* we want you to join us for a real crocodile hunt when we go out at night," they suggested. Somehow he never found the time.

Clyde Peters parachutes to Amazon jungle.

Clyde Peters with the *Fernando Stahl*.
At age 26, Clyde became the first full-time
Seventh-day Adventist missionary pilot.

The *Fernando Stahl*,
piloted by Clyde Peters.

Ready to jump!
Clyde volunteered to
jump into the jungle
to search for
survivors of a
LANSA Airline crash.

Happy children head for home after a day at the Shahuaya mission school.

Shipibo mother at Shahuaya carries her young daughter in a sling. After the tiny girl fell from a hut built high on poles to save the home during flood season, Clyde flew her out for medical help that saved her life.

Curious women from a nearby village watch as Clyde works on the plane at the home base in Yarina Cocha.

Eleanor helps Clyde move a plane. Clyde and Eleanor Peters worked together to keep the mission airbase going.

OB-M-

Schools like the Nevati mission school teach boys and girls to read and write in the official language of their country (Spanish). More importantly, children learn to love Jesus.

Marvin, Waloma, and son, Rick Fehrenbach. The Fehrenbachs operated the Nevati mission station, doing much to help in the early days of the mission aviation ministry.

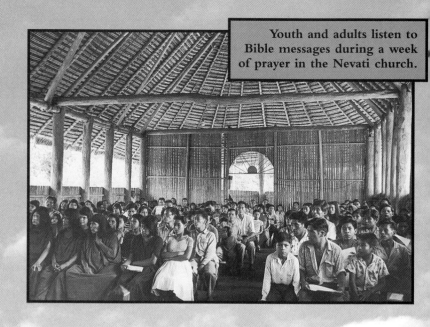

Youth and adults listen to Bible messages during a week of prayer in the Nevati church.

After a funeral service the body of a young mother is transported to burial grounds down the river. Death from unknown causes makes missionaries long for more medical expertise.

As a boy, Juan Ucayali was traded for a shotgun. Eventually he was released from slavery and found true freedom in the gospel of Jesus. He served as a mission translator at Nevati for many years.

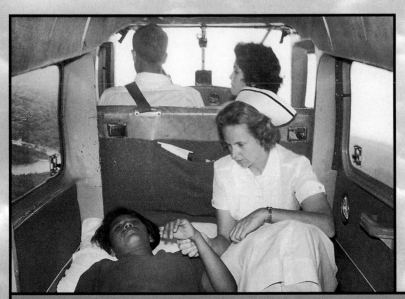

Clyde Peters saved many lives by using the mission plane to transport patients needing urgent medical treatment.

Siegfried Neuendorff, who studied tailoring as a youth in Germany, teaches a Campa woman to sew.

Chief Huánaco at Tisoventeni, a tribal leader in the wild Gran Pajonal, encouraged his people to allow the mission to start a school.

This Campa woman is an expert at spinning thread from wild cotton that grows in the jungle. The thread will be used to make the kind of clothing she is wearing.

Chief Huánaco (left) with two other Campa Indians.

Pastor Bob Seamount baptizes Marivanchi at Tsioventeni in the Gran Pajonal.

Chief Huánaco (center), leader of the Campas in the rugged Gran Pajonal, was unable to solve his problem of four wives. He has never been baptized but encouraged his son to be. Here, he discusses the school with fellow Campas.

Siegfried and Evelyn Neuendorff stand at the end of the runway with an Indian family at the Unini mission station.

Bob Seamount, former member of the King's Heralds Quartet, served with Clyde for several years in the Upper Amazon jungle. Shortly after he and Clyde ferried two mission planes to Africa, Elder Seamount was diagnosed with cancer and died within a few months.

This is the village of Amaquería, where the Shining Path guerillas determined to kill all the people for refusing to join in their fight against the government. Today 100 percent of the youth and adults have been baptized.

This candidate, being baptized by Bob Seamount, was prepared for baptism by Siegfried Neuendorff in the Unini mission station territory.

Clyde Peters (top center) and Alfredo Kalbermater (bottom left) spent several days diving in search of the *Fernando Stahl*, which sank when the river was at flood stage. No piece of the missing plane has ever been found.

Clyde extracts a tooth (one of more than 40,000 during his 10 years in the Upper Amazon jungle) beside the new *Fernando Stahl*, parked at the end of Amaquería's short runway, where the original *Fernando Stahl* sank in 100 feet of water. Miraculously, all in the plane got out without injury, even though the river was in flood.

The Doñez family. Augusto Doñez volunteered to work for the Chayawitas. His family's service of love resulted in hundreds of Chayawitas accepting Jesus.

Clyde brings the new *Fernando Stahl* in for a landing at the mission air base on the edge of Lake Yarina Cocha.

Tiny Nilda Bautista, sitting on her mother's lap, was one of the first patients whose life was saved after Clyde began his flying ministry in the upper Amazon.

The newest mission plane, the *James J. Aitken*, is flown by Alberto Marîn, the first Peruvian mission pilot. Alberto was baptized years ago by pastor Robert Seamount.

This three-toed sloth takes its time to climb a papaya tree in front of the Peters' home at Yarina Cocha.

Thanks to missions, these children at Nevati will be able to attend school as soon as they are old enough.

CHAPTER EIGHT

PICKET LINE AT PIPER

The Upper Amazon Mission invited Bob and Ellen Seamount to help meet the needs of an expanding air ministry. Bob, a pilot, pastor, and former member of the King's Herald Quartet, would direct the growing air program. Since no house was available, the Seamounts moved into a room in the hangar. With two pilots, another airplane became top priority. While the Seamounts were getting settled and studying Spanish, Clyde went to the States to pick up a Piper Cub. "I'll be back to Peru in a week," he told Bob.

Unfortunately, the Piper factory went on strike the morning Clyde arrived for the scheduled delivery. Picket lines had formed, blocking the release of any planes from the factory. *We urgently need the plane,* Clyde thought as he left the plant in disappointment. *What shall I do?* He asked himself. *I don't have time to waste.*

While waiting to decide what to do next, he went over to the nearby Lycoming Engine Plant and enrolled in an engine overhaul course. That took several days, but the strike at Piper continued. Later, while walking around the airport, he spotted William T. Piper himself. Clyde stepped up to the elderly Piper company founder and owner and introduced himself. "I'm a mission pilot from the Amazon jungle of Peru."

"Let's walk off to the side so I can hear more about your work," Mr. Piper suggested.

"Most jungle areas have no roads," Clyde explained. "By using a small plane we've opened up dozens of schools in remote areas where children have never had a chance to learn to read and write. When medical emergencies arise, we've used the plane to take in medical personnel or fly patients out to a hospital."

"I like what you're doing," the elderly man commented.

"We ordered a new Piper Cub," Peters explained, "and I came all the way from South America to pick it up. I've already been waiting for a week, and I really need to get back to my work in the jungle."

"This is a tough strike," Mr. Piper scowled. "It may last a long time. Give me a phone number where you can be reached. If there's anything I can do, I'll give you a call."

Later, back in his motel room, Clyde answered the phone. "Please meet me at the airport the first thing in the morning," the aircraft company owner requested. "Be sure to bring everything you need to take with you."

When the man arrived, he had all the paperwork for the purchased aircraft. "Your airplane is OBM 786. I'll tell you exactly where it is. Its tanks will have a few gallons of fuel."

They drove to the back of the Piper property next to the airport. Fifty acres of airplanes, surrounded by a high fence, sat wing-to-wing. Picketing continued on the factory side of the storage area.

"I may get into a lot of trouble for this," Piper said. "If you want this plane, you've got to get in it and fly it out." They stopped at a big gate. The factory owner sent an aid to open it, then handed Clyde the keys to the new aircraft. "You're on your own from here on out."

Clyde knew differently. *I'm not on my own,* he told himself. *The Lord's with me. This is the only plane to be delivered since the strike began more than a week ago.*

After checking the plane, Peters started the engine and taxied down between rows of new planes. He increased power, and with a light load of fuel the new Super Cub lifted off the ground in seconds and turned away from the strikers determined to keep the plant closed.

Amazing, Clyde thought. *Mr. Piper said big corporations offered large sums of money to have their plane delivered, and his factory managers refused to take the risk, but he personally risked delivering a plane for God's work in Peru.*

He flew to the nearest airport, 20 miles away, filled his tanks, and took off for Lincoln, Nebraska. Old friends helped him install radio and navigation equipment and a 60-gallon belly tank for additional fuel. With everything ready, he headed straight to Peru, arriving in time for a Youth Congress being conducted on the campus of Inca Union College.

The little Piper Cub, equipped with large tundra tires, landed on the college farm. A special ceremony dedicated the plane with the name *Ricardo Hayden* in honor of pioneer missionaries, Elder and Mrs. Richard Hayden, who had joined the Stahls at the Amazon headwaters in 1931.

Following the dedication, Clyde piloted the tiny *Ricardo Hayden* up over the Andes to the air base near Pucallpa. "God worked a miracle," he told Eleanor. "Without the kindness of Mr. Piper, I'd still be waiting for the plane. With two planes, Bob and I will be able to take the gospel to many new areas."

About this time, a band of guerrilla terrorists inspired by Che Guevara plagued the jungle city of Satípo. They blew up a bank, stole money from businesses, and shot civilians. The terrorists fled when the president of Peru sent commandos to stop the violence.

In hot pursuit, the soldiers flew to Puerto Bermudez and took a boat up the Pachitea River to the Nevati Mission Station. Bad weather grounded Clyde and the *Ricardo Hayden* at Nevati the evening they arrived.

The commandos believed the terrorists had escaped into the rugged Gran Pajonal and carried a map showing all the Adventist airstrips. Their leader approached Clyde. "*Capitán* Peters, you are to fly us into the Gran Pajonal tomorrow morning. This is not a request, it's an order. Do you understand?"

Clyde eyed the men, heavily armed with automatic weapons and plenty of ammunition. *This is the last thing I want to do.* He faced a perplexing situation. *If I fly commandos in and they start shooting, some of our new believers may get caught in the cross fire. What will they think, knowing the killers came in the mission plane?*

"You know," Clyde said, "I'm here now because Nevati is socked in with bad weather. Who knows what it will be like tomorrow. You may not be going any place."

In the meantime, Clyde consulted with the mission station director. "We'll be in trouble if we don't accommodate these men sent by the government, yet we may have problems if we do." They both agreed, though, that the better judgment would be to provide the transportation.

Before going to bed Clyde prayed, "Lord, please give us bad weather if You don't want me to fly the commandos. I want to do Your will."

At dawn, Clyde looked out toward the Gran Pajonal—he could see all the way back into the Andes. "The sky is crystal clear," he told the commandos. "I'll take you, but please be careful around the Adventist villages. We don't want any of our people injured."

Three men, carrying pistols, hand grenades, and automatic weapons squeezed into the back of the plane. Clyde had already filled the fuel tanks to maximum capacity. As the sun rose, they took off toward the Gran Pajonal. Suddenly, two miles out a temperature and dew point situation developed, turning the clear atmosphere into a blanket of dense fog.

In seconds, Peters began flying on instruments. He turned and started to lose altitude, hoping to find his way back to Nevati. With no sign of the river he had just flown over, he said, "It's impossible to fly back to Nevati. I'm going to climb out over this fog and head for Oventeni in the Gran Pajonal."

Still inside a thick cloud after an hour of flying, he calculated by the instruments that they were near Oventeni. For half an hour Clyde searched for openings to land but found none. "We've been flying for 1 and a half hours," he told the soldiers. "You can see the situation we're in. In all my years of flying I've never seen dense clouds form so fast. We'll fly over to the Perené. It's always open over there."

They soared for another hour over a solid sea of clouds. Clyde climbed up to 9,000 feet—still heavy fog. He turned to the men, "I've got to turn around. There are high mountains ahead. We don't dare fly around mountains when we can't see. We'll go to the Ucayali River on the eastern side of the Andes and try to land at Unini."

Another hour and no sign of Unini. "We must be over the Ucayali," Clyde reported, "but with no radio beacons or navigational aids of any kind, I can't be sure."

"We don't want to die, *Capitán* Peters!" the commandoes pleaded. "Please get us back on the ground." What should have been a 20-minute flight on a clear day had already lasted two and a half hours flying on instruments without a single crack in the clouds.

"The best thing we can do is to fly back over the Perené,"

Clyde said. "It's later now and we should find some breaks." He glanced back as three pale-faced men took out their crucifixes, crossed themselves, and prayed. Clyde smiled. "You'd better pray! This unusual weather has put us in a very serious situation."

I appreciate their prayers, Clyde thought, *but it's almost comical.* One man, sure he would die, prayed out loud, "Oh Lord, forgive me for the way I've treated my mother."

Clyde crossed back over the Gran Pajonal. "Listen, men, we've flown three hours now and the plane carries fuel for only four. There's a small village northwest of Satípo where the real high Andes begin."

The commandos, in the back of the plane with their automatic weapons, cried like babies. Clyde silently prayed, "Lord, our fuel is getting low and I'm not coming up with answers. I've tried every way I know to find a clearing where we can get down out of the clouds and land. Nothing's worked. We're dangerously close to the mountains. It's time for You to take over."

Turning to the terrified men, Clyde said, "Keep praying. God knows how to get this plane back on the ground."

The air was smooth, but with absolute zero visibility. Five minutes later they encountered a hole 200 feet wide that opened up like a big funnel in the clouds. Directly below lay an airstrip. When Clyde banked the plane, he couldn't find the opening again. "Dear Lord, I still need your help. Please help me find the way down to the ground."

In seconds he saw the hole, cut the power, and put the plane in a 90° spiral. The commandos screamed as if they were going out of their minds. The little plane pulled out under the clouds and Clyde put it gently down on the dirt runway. Three armed men jumped out, bent down, and kissed the ground.

"We'll sit here till the weather clears," Clyde announced.

The commandos had another idea. "We're going to stay right here. We don't want to fly any more." The men who had shortly before prayed for their very lives now marched off to a tavern and got so drunk they couldn't stand up.

Clyde waited on the runway. *God controls the weather—even the clouds obey Him. We didn't get in trouble with the government by refusing to transport these men. And we didn't land in the Gran Pajonal where they could have caused problems for our work.*

Flying home after the weather cleared that afternoon, Clyde thought of the need to keep up to date with his skydiving skills.

He talked with Bob. "I haven't jumped for a long time. There may be an emergency when I'll need to use my parachute. As the only pilot at the base, I couldn't jump, but with you here, I'd like to practice jumping."

"Good idea, Clyde," Bob said. "You know, we have camp meetings scheduled for Nevati and Unini. The mission station directors could announce that you'll jump out of an airplane and that could create interest and increase the attendance."

At Nevati Clyde jumped just after a late afternoon meeting. Horrified Campas hid their faces, sure he would end up splattered on the ground. Then they leaped and laughed when the parachute opened and he floated down out of the sky, landing right on target. Pastors explained how exciting it will be when Jesus comes down through the eastern sky at the Second Coming.

At Unini, Siegfried spread the word that Clyde would jump out of a plane during its camp meeting. Indians living in distant villages walked for days to reach the mission station.

Three years had passed since the *Fernando Stahl* first landed in the Gran Pajonal. Marivanchi, the wife of the chief at Tsioventeni, was one of the first persons Bob Seamount baptized after arriving in Peru. Her husband, Shawingo, wanted to be baptized, but he had two wives. At last he chose to keep his first wife, Marivanchi, and let the younger woman go. Turning from witchcraft, he stopped sipping tobacco juice, then prayed to the God of heaven for forgiveness for murdering four men.

Shawingo guided the Tsioventeni group on the long journey over a rugged trail to the Unini camp meeting. At mealtime he always led his people in saying the blessing for the food. Every morning at 6:00 a.m. the Indians conducted prayer bands, impressing the missionaries with the fact that all the children from Tsioventeni knew how to pray.

At noon on Friday Clyde surprised the camp meeting crowd by parachuting to the Unini airstrip. The next day the worshipers rejoiced when Shawingo, chief of Tsioventeni, was baptized in the Unini River. Oscar, son of Chief Huánaco from the Gran Pajonal, followed Jesus in baptism too. On Sunday Bob Seamount flew into Tsioventeni and baptized 10 more.

Sometime later, the mayor of Yurimaguas, a jungle city with more than 50,000 inhabitants, planned a centennial celebration and contacted the local pastor. "We want Adventists to take part as we commemorate the founding of our city. Besides

having fireworks, we've invited many organizations to partici-
pate and want Adventists to do something spectacular."

The request perplexed Pastor Alomía. He asked his wife,
"What can our church do for a big worldly celebration like this?"

Then they got an idea and sent a telegram to the Adventist
air base. "We want Clyde Peters to do a parachute jump for the
Yurimaguas Centennial." Peters talked it over with Seamont.
Their work had been limited to reaching tribes. Although not a
normal activity, here was a chance to do something in a city and
give its people opportunity to hear about Seventh-day Adventists.

People came from everywhere—more than 100,000
crowded into the streets. At the edge of town 40,000 jammed
the stadium for a soccer game. "Senor Peters, I want you to
jump into the stadium," the mayor said.

Bob flew to 10,000 feet and Clyde, with a 100 pound sack
of flour, dove out of the *Ricardo Hayden,* leaving a beautiful
white streak in the sky. The game on the ground stopped as
everyone looked up. Peruvians love their red and white flag. At
about 2,000 feet Clyde pulled his rip cord and a brilliant red and
white parachute popped open.

Crowds yelled and screamed as Clyde turned and floated
over the field twice, then turned again and landed in the mid-
dle of the stadium. Thousands of people poured out of town toward the stadium and spectators in the bleachers rushed to the
playing field. The police found themselves powerless to hold
them back. The crowd surrounded Clyde, pushing closer and
closer. He struggled to stand up. "Lord," he prayed, "save me
from being crushed to death!"

The huge crowds outside hit the stadium wall and it crum-
bled like paper. *This crazy mob is out of control! Everyone wants to
touch me.* The excited mass of people knocked Clyde down and
trampled on him. He wrestled to get up again and finally managed to pull the parachute into his arms.

As he walked to Pastor Alomía's house, 50,000 people
jammed the streets behind him. That evening the mayor visited
Peters and Seamont. "I'm sorry about the problem today," he
said. "Several hundred men are working all night to repair the
stadium. We want you to jump again tomorrow. The red and
white parachute falling out of a blue sky is the greatest thing that
ever happened to our city."

When the mayor promised more security to control the

crowds, Clyde agreed to jump again. The next morning the stadium filled to capacity and thousands more crowded outside. Climbing to 10,000 feet for another spectacular jump, Clyde chatted with Seamont. "I wonder what this city was like 100 years ago."

"Probably only a few people," Bob commented.

"One thing sure, there were no Adventists. Pioneer missionaries like the Stahls and Haydens hadn't come to Peru yet. Now, because of the work they started, we have more than 4,000 believers in the upper Amazon."

Leaving Bob and the plane, Clyde dove through the sky and opened his 'chute, allowing the bright morning sun to break through the red and white canopy. Then in horror he watched as the mass of people below became out of control again. The mayor's security forces were no match for the excited crowd. Clyde crossed over the stadium twice as people applauded, then turned and landed outside. The people inside the stadium pushed the walls down, totally demolishing the wooden structure as they tried to reach him on the outside.

Clyde, anxious to get back to the plane and fly home with Bob, pulled the parachute into his arms and raced ahead of the crowd all the way to the airport. The mayor came to thank them for the Adventist participation in the celebration. "Don't worry about the stadium," he said. "We'll build a better one. In 100 years, our city has never experienced anything like your parachute jumps."

CHAPTER NINE

MONSTER AT MIDNIGHT

Alfredo Kalbermater, always ready to help with any need, gave outstanding support to the air base program. As nurses, he and his wife, Flora, treated the patients who came to the hangar for medical care. Also, Alfredo helped maintain the mission planes. Clyde Peters could call him anytime, day or night, even at 1:00 in the morning, and he would jump up and come without complaint.

Each time Alfredo fueled an airplane, he poured the gasoline through a chamois. He and others took every precaution to make sure the fuel used in the mission planes remained contamination free. The base purchased aviation fuel in Lima, sealed it in 55-gallon drums, and shipped it over the Andes by truck. Someone from the base always went and checked the barrels to make sure they were clean before being filled. After a few years, they began to trust the supplier and didn't always take the precaution.

Early one morning, Clyde took the *Ricardo Hayden* and headed for Chesea on the border of Brazil. "I should follow the river," he radioed the base, "but I can save a lot of time by cutting across a swamp. It doesn't matter if it's 10 feet or 100 feet deep, I know it's not a good place to swim. The super cub engine is running great and a shortcut will save money for the mission."

Halfway across the swamp, the engine coughed and started running rough. Immediately Clyde checked his instruments. An increased exhaust temperature indicated a problem with the fuel mixture. He used full throttle to open the power enrichment valve in the carburetor. The temperature dropped, then began rising again.

Back on the radio, Clyde tried to speak calmly. "I shouldn't have tried this! The engine's acting up and I'm heading for Amaquería, 15 miles away on the Ucayali River." Then he added carburetor heat—another way to enrich the fuel mixture.

He approached Amaquería with full power and carburetor heat on. The exhaust temperature rose higher and higher. *This engine's going to quit!* It ran so poorly that he cut the power and glided in on the short runway.

Safe on the ground, Clyde jumped out, removed the cowling, and pushed the quick drain. Fuel ran out. "This feels strange," he told the people who crowded around the plane. Taking out the sediment bulb and a filter screen, he held it up and blew on it. "It feels sticky—like drying lacquer. There's something in the fuel."

"What can we do to help?" the mission teachers asked.

"Let's have the women bring all their biggest containers—pots, pans, kettles—anything that will hold gasoline."

Clyde drained all the fuel from both tanks into the women's containers. After all the sticky stuff settled to the bottom of the pans, he collected the clean fuel, poured it back into the plane's tanks, sloshed it around, and let it flow out again. After six hours of work he had collected more than a gallon of material that looked like thick mucus. With the filter cleaned and the fuel back in the tanks, the engine started and ran well. Clyde thanked the Shipibos at Amaquería for letting him use their containers and flew straight to Pucallpa. "The Lord helped me today," he reported on the radio. "I came close to going down in a swamp where I could not have survived."

Back at the base, he called all the personnel to the hanger. "We've got a problem, men. Let's check all our fuel barrels." The first one they examined was the one they had used to fill the tanks before his morning flight. It contained big globs of gooey gunk. Soon they found another barrel contaminated with the same sticky stuff.

"It's amazing," Clyde said, "how this stuff slips right through a chamois with no indication of a problem. From now on we're going to follow new guidelines to make sure we never purchase contaminated fuel again."

The United States donated a twin engine Albatross to the Peruvian Air Force, a plane loaded with expensive electronic equipment for locating submarines. Peru wanted to use the plane to give pilots amphibious training. Instead of practicing in the salty Pacific, the Peruvian air force brought the aircraft to Yarina Cocha and began practicing takeoffs and landings in fresh water near the Adventist air base.

One day Clyde worked in the hangar to complete a 100 hour inspection on the *Fernando Stahl*. While tightening a nut, he heard a strange sound out on the lake—"unrrrrrrrr!" Dropping his wrench, he glanced out. A plane floated on the water, but with aircraft taking off and landing all the time he saw no reason for alarm.

"Should I go check on this?" he asked a worker. He reached the front of the hangar just as the Albatross nosed over and flopped up on it's back. Racing to the lake's edge, Clyde arrived in time to see the pilot and trainees get out of the plane without injury. The cabin, mostly submerged, quickly filled with water. The pilot, seeing Clyde, said, "All of our luggage is still inside the plane."

"Maybe I can help," Peters responded. "I just bought a scuba air tank, regulator, and mask. I don't have any diving experience, but I'll get my equipment and see what I can do."

After retrieving all the crew's personal luggage, he towed the Albatross up in front of the mission air base. During the night, a windstorm blew the plane back out into the lake where it sank in 100 feet of water.

Dwight Taylor, a certified scuba diver serving as youth director for the Upper Amazon Mission, learned about the accident during a radio conversation with Eleanor Peters. He went to Peruvian Air Force offices in Iquitos and volunteered his services. The next day they flew him and his diving equipment to Yarina Cocha.

Air force officers came from Lima and asked the Adventist air base for help. "We have more than US$600,000 worth of radio and radar equipment in that plane, and we would like to have you get it out for us."

"With Dwight here to show us how to use our equipment properly," Clyde said, "we'll do our best." They rigged up sealed beam lights to use under water. Clyde, Alfredo, and Dwight dove down together.

At first they felt very uneasy trying to orient themselves in the spooky environment of a plane laying upside down on the bottom of a lake. Soon, though, the men adjusted to the underwater conditions and each time they surfaced with a piece of equipment, an officer congratulated them. When they emerged with a piece of highly-confidential electronics, the officer's face glowed, "You men are doing a great job."

At the end of the day, the Peruvian officials announced, "We have the most important things now and we're going to take them back to Lima. You may work more if you wish."

By the time they finished removing all the navigation instruments, the plane seemed to be floating. Air exhaled from their diving masks had become trapped in the plane. The next day they rigged up a compressor, pumped in more air, and the plane drifted to the surface.

Tying the plane to a canoe with an outboard motor, they towed it half a mile back to the front of the air base property. After working several days, Dwight returned to his work at mission headquarters. Clyde had flights to make and Alfredo wanted to keep up with his responsibilities.

"When I'm home on weekends," Clyde told Alfredo, "I'll work on the Albatross for Saturday night recreation."

"Don't leave me out," Alfredo volunteered. "I'll help all I can." Many times they went out Saturday night after sunset and worked until 11:00 or 12:00 p.m.

"We need to get the plane out of the water so we can salvage the landing gear and hydraulic system," the air force officers announced when they returned.

"Before we can do that for you," Clyde explained, "we'll have to figure out a way to turn the plane over and get it right side up. But we'll try."

They towed it back out into the lake. Using a winch and cable, they flipped the plane over, only to watch in horror as it sank. To refloat the plane, they tied deflated life rafts, strapped them under the wings, and refilled them with air—but it was not enough. Next they strapped 55-gallon drums under the plane and filled them with air. But each time they expected the Albatross to float, something went wrong.

They knew that the Indians living along the lake believed an old legend about a huge monster living in Yarina Cocha. The beast could swallow a canoe full of Indians in one gulp. Because of this tale, some were afraid to travel on the lake at night. When a large fresh water porpoise jumped out in front of a canoe at night, it took a strong person not to get frightened.

"Let's pump compressed air directly into the chambers inside the plane," Clyde finally suggested. The idea worked too well. The plane shot to the surface, dumping over the canoe with their compressor. By the time they retrieved the compressor from the bottom of the lake, the plane they had just floated sank again, so they quit for the night.

About midnight the next Saturday night, the men stood in an air chamber with their masks off. They'd been pumping air into the sunken plane. It began to move. "Alfredo," Clyde shouted, "get your mask on!"

Peters swam to the surface to get the canoe with the compressor out of the way. After paddling the canoe load of equipment off to the side, he stopped to look around. *What a marvelous Amazon night!* A full moon reflected on the lake's mirror-like surface.

A *peckypeck* full of drunk Indians returning from a party chugged by just as the Albatross popped to the surface. These natives froze as they saw a huge monster rise out of the lake with water spouting from its sides and tail. The tail flipped up, then the plane dove back down into the lake. Because the men saw it with their own eyes under a full moon at midnight, they were convinced that the Yarina Cocha monster was real. The legend revived.

The Albatross had pitched as it rose to the surface. Air moved around in the different bays, pushing water out over the bulkheads, and blowing water out through a tube in the tail. The plane sank again with Alfredo still inside. He surfaced and found Clyde sitting in the canoe, doubled over with laughter.

The men spent more Saturday nights and several tries before successfully floating the plane right side up. Then they used a tractor to pull it out onto a concrete ramp, ready to turn over to the Peruvian Air Force. Their efforts created a great deal of goodwill for Adventist missions.

During his frequent flights to Unini, Clyde made special friends with a Campa boy named Moisés. The mission school student was the one who almost always found Bible texts first at Sabbath afternoon youth meetings. He was also the kind of fellow who enjoyed doing more than his share of work.

The Unini Mission Station sits on a high bank facing the airstrip on the opposite side of the river. Every time Clyde landed at Unini, Moisés, cutting grass on the runway with a machete, was the first person he would see. His hair would be flying in every direction and he'd have a great big smile.

Moisés could take six or seven people with their baggage across the river in a dugout canoe. He would grab a long pole and push the canoe up along the riverbank to just the right spot. Then, shoving the canoe out into the swift current, he would land on the opposite shore exactly at the path leading to the mission station.

Clyde marveled at the boy's skill. "Will you let me try this?" he asked one day.

"Sure, *Capitán*," the boy grinned. The whole village came out to watch. Everyone laughed when Clyde fell out of the canoe. After turning the canoe over half a dozen times, he gave up and let Moisés transport him across the river.

Late one afternoon, Clyde, back at the base, heard the radio begin to crackle. Evelyn Neuendorff called from Unini. "Urgent! Please send the airplane immediately. A *shushupie* jumped up and bit Moisés on the shoulder while he was cutting grass on the runway. He's screaming with horrendous pain. His shoulder, arm, and chest have turned black."

He's my favorite Campa boy, Clyde thought as he listened. *He's a real Christian.*

"It's getting dark," he answered. "We're not allowed to fly at night so I'll fly to Unini the first thing in the morning." Clyde knew that a *shushupie* (fer-de-lance) is the most poisonous snake in South America. When one of the snakes sinks its fangs in a human, the bite is usually fatal.

A doctor from Loma Linda was visiting the air base. Clyde took him into Pucallpa and they bought the best antivenim available. Alfredo fueled the plane while Clyde fixed a bed in the back of the *Fernando Stahl*. Unini called again. "Moisés is getting worse."

"We'll keep praying," Clyde promised. "I'm bringing a doctor, and we'll be there the first thing in the morning."

Determined to do everything possible to save the boy's life, Clyde and the doctor boarded the plane before sunrise. "The snakebite patient's the kind of cheerful Christian every church needs," he told the doctor as they quickly taxied to the end of the runway. Then suddenly fog immersed them. "This is not what we need, but I've got to get the antivenim to Moisés."

Without consulting anyone by radio, Clyde took off. At 300 feet they came out on top. Fog covered the jungle as far as they could see. "Don't worry doctor," he said, "I'll fly just east of the Gran Pajonal Range. There's got to be a break in the clouds so we can land at Unini."

Immediately after takeoff, Unini radioed the air base. "Please cancel the plane. Moisés is walking around in good shape. His arm doesn't hurt at all." The base flipped the frequency to single side band and called the *Fernando Stahl*. Strangely, the radio in the plane didn't respond.

Clyde recognized every nook and cranny in the mountains. After about an hour, he said, "We're over Unini, but it's still covered with fog." He turned toward the Ucayali, slowed the plane, and, watching for treetops, started to let down. "Oh, thank you, Lord," he breathed a prayer when the Ucayali River appeared below the fog.

Back at the air base the radio clattered to life again. "Moisés just dropped dead," Unini reported. "He felt fine, we canceled the plane, now he's dead." The base tried to reach Clyde in the *Fernando Stahl* but still received no response.

Clyde skimmed under the fog over the Ucayali to the mouth of the Unini, then headed up river toward the mission station. Fog, however, dropped right down to the water, forcing him to do a 180° turn. The doctor, sensing danger, wished he had stayed back at the base.

"If I go up through the fog, I may not get back down." He flew low, barely above the river. "The only other place I can land is at Chicosa, down river from Unini. A Baptist missionary built a runway near his home."

Rounding a bend, Clyde climbed a little to get on the runway, and landed with fog only 50 feet above the ground. Everyone in the village ran out to meet the plane. The Baptist missionary pushed through the crowd, "My wife's dying," he said, trembling. "She's terribly sick, and we have been praying for a plane. With all the fog, we were sure a plane could not come."

"I've got the best doctor in the country right here," Clyde spoke encouragingly. "We have a bed all made up in the back of the plane."

The husband, worn out from being up all night with his extremely sick wife, listened in amazement. "It's a miracle the way God has answered our prayers."

"Get your wife ready! The doctor will look at her and we'll fly just as soon as the fog lifts. I have to make a short stop in Unini, then we'll fly straight on to Pucallpa."

By the time they could get the sick woman in the plane, the fog ceiling lifted from 50 feet to almost 400. Clyde flew to Unini. Not having received the radio messages, he broke down and wept when they told him Moisés was dead.

All the way back to Pucallpa, he tried to figure it out. "Why? Why? Why did God let the boy die?" Clyde questioned. "I've got to believe God knows best. Certainly Moisés was ready. He was a beautiful Christian boy. God's Word is true: 'Blessed are the dead who die in the Lord (Rev. 14:13, RSV).'"

Appropriate medical care at the hospital in Pucallpa saved the missionary wife, and after a few days Clyde flew her back home. "Two things happened when your husband prayed for a plane," he told the woman. "First the radio in my plane failed to function when the base tried to call and cancel my flight. Then the Lord created a weather situation forcing me to land here at Chicosa."

Flying back to the mission base, he prayed, "Thank You for using a Seventh-day Adventist mission plane to answer a Baptist missionary's prayer."

Clyde remembered how as a boy he had first learned about Jesus in the little Baptist church his parents attended in Kansas. He felt grateful to God for opportunities to serve people of all faiths.

CHAPTER TEN

UNBUCKLE YOUR SEAT BELTS!

Clyde's parents, Melvin and Georgianna Peters, arrived in Peru to spend a few weeks assisting the aviation ministry. Melvin made repairs around the base while Georgianna, a registered nurse, helped the Kalbermater's care for patients who came to the jungle hangar for treatment. Bob Seamount worked out a schedule for Clyde to take his whole family to visit six villages up the Ucayali River. They would conduct meetings and provide medical attention.

Early on a February morning they prepared to leave. When Clyde went in for breakfast, his dad, waiting at the table questioned, "Would you be content to go back to a Kansas wheat farm after what you're doing here?"

"You know, Dad," his son answered, "I was never crazy about the farm."

Melvin looked at him. "I always hoped you could take over the farm when I get too old to work it anymore."

"Sell it, Dad. This is where I belong. I'm doing something worthwhile for the Lord—nothing else interests me."

When the rest of the family came to the table, Clyde reached for his Bible. "Let's have worship before we eat." He prayed for the mission work in the Amazon jungle and for Bob who had flown out earlier in the *Ricardo Hayden*. Then he asked the Lord to bless his family as they flew to Ucayali villages. Amaquería would be their first stop.

After breakfast, he began loading the plane. Six emergency life jackets had hung in the *Fernando Stahl*, but thieves had stolen them during a recent trip to mission headquarters in Iquitos. *Oh, well,* Clyde thought, *We're doing short flights. Since the airplane engine is in top condition, we won't be needing them.*

With the equipment loaded, his whole family—father, mother, wife, and three children—climbed into the *Fernando Stahl*. The Seamount's still lived in the hangar and Bob's wife, Ellen, watched them load. After a few moments she walked up to the plane, "Clyde, you've got too much weight!"

"Yeah," he said, "we're a little heavy—but this plane's built to take big loads."

"Too much weight!" she persisted.

Clyde resented Mrs. Seamont's caution and silently reasoned, *Her husband's one of the finest men I've ever worked with, but she needs to understand that I'm responsible for this flight.*

The powerful *Fernando Stahl* lifted off the air base runway without difficulty. Clyde flew up the Ucayali River and touched down on the short airstrip at Amaquería. There he set up equipment to extract teeth. Grandma Peters and Eleanor gave medication to a tuberculosis patient and treated other medical needs. Grandpa Peters set up the projector and generator for use at the evening program.

Indians packed the thatched chapel at meeting time. Clyde and the older children played trumpets accompanied by Eleanor on her accordion. Dad Peters showed a film. Then Eleanor illustrated a Bible story with her flannelgraph. Finally Clyde opened his Bible and talked about the soon coming of Jesus.

The villagers had provided a hut where the Peters' family could use their air mattresses and sleep under mosquito nets. Gentle rain began falling on the palm thatched roof. Happy thoughts filled Clyde's mind as he drifted off to sleep. *Mom and Dad don't fuss at me any more about flying. It's wonderful to have them here to help our family bring the gospel to these remote areas.*

He slept through the rain that fell most of the night. Before breakfast, they held another meeting. After eating, Clyde loaded the plane and prepared to fly to the next village. Amaquería has a one-way landing strip. Tall trees stand at one end and the riverbank at the other. A plane must fly in over the river and stop before reaching the trees. To take off, it starts against the trees and flies out over the river.

Clyde, knowing how heat and humidity affect the power of an engine, taxied as close to the trees as possible. Atmospheric conditions affect lift from the wings and the efficiency of the propeller, so he wanted to use the maximum length of the short runway. The air appeared calm, with perhaps a two or three mile an hour tail wind. His family bowed their heads as Clyde prayed for God's protection. Before adding power, he asked, "Does everyone have their seatbelt fastened?"

The weather ahead looked great, but a rain shower moved in from the mountains. The *Fernando Stahl* picked up speed while they waved to grateful villagers lining the runway. *Something's terribly wrong*, Clyde thought as the plane reached the last 150 feet of the runway. *We've stopped gaining speed and have already passed the point of no return! It's too late to abort take off!*

The plane flew off the end of the runway where the bank usually dropped 40 or 50 feet to the water's edge. With the Ucayali at flood stage, the water level rose to within two feet of the top of the bank. The wheels skimmed like skis on top of the water. The plane started to rise, then settled down like a duck on the swollen river. The swift current carried floating logs and debris. Whirlpools swirled around the plane.

"Unbuckle your seat belts!" Clyde ordered. They were the only words he spoke inside the sinking plane. Seven-year-old Alan and 8-year-old Shelly sat on their grandfather's lap. Alan held his nose as water rose to the instrument panel. The plane's nose plunged from the weight of the engine and the *Fernando Stahl* flipped over on it's back.

Stunned, no one had unbuckled. They all hung upside down. The muddy river swept around them, turning the cabin dark. Clyde worked to get his seat belt off. *My mother can't swim, 5-year-old Linda can't swim. I've got to get everybody out.*

All his efforts to force the door open, though, failed. Suddenly the plane rolled to the left, the door popped open, and water rushed in. He grabbed Shelly and Allen and swam to the surface. *Dad's buckled up in the plane*, Clyde thought. *What if he can't get his seat belt unhooked?*

Grandma Peters, Eleanor, and little Linda were all in the back seat. As the plane had dropped into the river, Georgianna Peters thought, *This is the end, but at least our family's together.* "Lord, please forgive my sins," she prayed. "I want to be ready with all my family when You come." She grabbed her granddaughter, Linda, as the aircraft rolled over.

How long will it take to drown? Eleanor wondered at the same moment.

After Clyde opened his door, more water poured in, building pressure on the inside of the plane. The pilot's side of the plane dipped deeper into the water, swinging Eleanor's door up near the surface. She opened it and climbed out, followed by Grandma Peters.

Although Shelly and Alan swam almost every day in Lake Yarina Cocha, they had no experience swimming in a raging river filled with whirlpools and rapids. Clyde stayed close to them. "You better slow down and not wear yourselves out," he shouted.

"There's Dad," he said, glancing back. "Thank the Lord, he got out!"

Georgianna Peters clung to a piece of the plane sticking out of the water and screamed, "Melvin, I can't swim."

She grabbed a plastic water jug. When a trumpet case floated to the surface, her husband yelled, "Georgianna, grab that trumpet case!" As the last piece of the *Fernando Stall* disappeared in the muddy river, Grandmother Peters tried to stay afloat by holding the trumpet case under one arm and the water jug under the other.

Eleanor looked around to make sure everyone was there. "Where's Linda? Linda? Where's Linda?"

"I had her in my arms in the plane," Grandma Peters yelled, "but I lost her on the way out."

Seconds later, the child popped out of the water and hit her mother's chin. Eleanor breathed a prayer, "Thank You, Lord, for putting Linda in my arms."

Clyde, with the two older children, kept fighting to reach shore as his father followed. Eleanor struggled to support Linda. *I can't keep this up much longer,* she thought. Just as she was about ready to give up, the flannel board floated by. She and Linda both grabbed it. The wooden board holding the flannel had just enough buoyancy to keep them from going under.

The Shipibo Indians had watched in horror when the mission plane splashed into the water and sank. Strong men raced for their canoes, grabbed paddles, and pushed out into the swift current. Grandma Peters watched the men paddle out and pick up Clyde, Alan, and Shelly. Then they rescued her husband. Finally they reached Eleanor and Linda and pulled them into the canoe.

Since Georgianna couldn't swim, the swift current carried

her far down the river. The trumpet case became waterlogged and she fought to keep her face above water. Sometimes she swept past whirlpools big enough to swallow her. She shut her eyes when the current tried to pull her under.

I'm thankful, she thought. *Clyde's family is safe. They just picked Melvin up. But me, I'll never make it. They won't reach me in time. I'm an old woman so it doesn't matter.*

Thoughts of despair plagued her, yet she clung desperately to the soggy trumpet case and water jug. Her arms ached. Again and again she tried to turn the jug over so she could hold on to it by the handle, but each time she failed.

At last, a canoe pulled alongside her. An Indian reached down to pull her up. Unfortunately, his hand slipped and she sank beneath the water. The next thing she remembered was that she was now inside the canoe. Her plastic water jug sat by the trumpet case and water ran out into the canoe. Suddenly it dawned upon her, *God kept me from turning the jug over because it doesn't have a lid. If I'd held it upright as I wanted to, it would have filled with water and I would have drowned.*

Because they had drifted far down river, their Indian rescuers transferred the Peters to a larger canoe with a motor. Feeling sick in his stomach, Clyde scanned the Ucayali. "There's no sign of any part of the plane." He felt as if a big chunk of his heart had gone to the bottom of the river with the *Fernando Stahl.*

Indians wept as the canoe docked at Amaquería. Suffering shock over what had just happened, Clyde and his family, water dripping from their wet clothes, walked directly to the little thatched church and knelt together on the dirt floor. Saddened for the loss of the plane, but also shedding tears of joy, they thanked God for having saved them from a river grave.

"Dear Lord," Clyde prayed, "please watch over the plane and help us find it so it can fly again." Then excusing himself, he walked alone down Amaquería's short runway. *I should have done this before trying to take off,* he thought. *God didn't want us to lose a plane. I must learn the lesson He wants to teach me. Pride kept me from listening to Ellen when she told me we were too heavy. Sure, the Helio Courier can take heavy loads, but not under these conditions.*

Clyde hadn't noticed, but the Indians reported a strong gust of tail wind just as the plane took off. When he walked on down the runway he saw the real reason for the accident. The landing gear left tracks six to eight inches deep in soft mud in the last 150 feet where he failed to pick up speed.

Why didn't I check the runway? He kept asking himself.

God knows that pilots are human. Clyde had landed there the day before and everything had been fine. With the river at flood stage and a night of rain, the last part of the runway had become water logged and dangerous without him realizing it.

Clyde took a canoe down river to Caco where a missionary group had a radio. He called for Bob Seamount to pick them up. Bob arrived in the *Ricardo Hayden*. Wanting Clyde to regain his confidence, he said, "Here, you fly this plane." Two trips brought every one safely back to the air base.

All their personal belongings, even toothbrushes, had gone to the bottom of the river. Five-year-old Linda searched the house, found one old toothbrush, and cleaned it up. She sang over and over to her doll, "What do you know? What do you know? My grandpa and my grandma, my daddy and my mommy and Shelly and Alan and Linda—we have only one toothbrush."

The next day Bob and Clyde flew back to Amaquería with diving equipment. They borrowed a boat, paddled out, and dropped an anchor in the swift current. It sank a long way down. When it finally hit bottom, the current whipped them around and they nearly lost the boat. Donning diving gear, Clyde started down the rope. A strong current lashed at him as he clung desperately to the rope. Twenty feet down the current ripped off his oxygen mask and he had to fight his way back to the surface.

Seeing the danger, Seamont declared, "The plane can be replaced, but we can never replace you. We'll give up on this for now."

Clyde agreed, but on the flight back to Pucallpa he said, "Our family has vacation plans, but they're changing. When the rainy season ends and the river goes down, I'm spending my vacation searching for the *Fernando Stahl*.

Bob Seamount, the air base director, raised the question in his official report: "Was the plane overloaded? The answer is no. There was a fairly heavy load, but well within the weight and balance limits." Clyde wanted to take the blame as "pilot error."

A few days later Peters received a telegram signed by Roger Wilcox, president, and M. S. Nigri, secretary of the South American Division. "GRATEFUL GOD'S PROTECTION,

CONTINUED CONFIDENCE IN AIR PROGRAM." Clyde deeply appreciated the understanding church leaders.

A report filled out for the mission flights during the three years of the *Fernando Stahl's* service included the following:

4,000 flights (average flight 22½ minutes)

63 lives saved by emergency flights

21,163 persons given medical service

23,200 teeth extracted

48,400 pounds of food hauled to flood victims

17,000 passengers—pastors, teachers, and mission personnel

Many years before, Pastor F. A. Stahl had dashed down swift rapids on a raft with Indian guides. The raft struck a submerged log and flipped over, pinning Stahl underneath. He was able to free himself and swim out along with his companions. The airplane named in his honor was not so fortunate.

During the dry season, with the river at its lowest, Clyde, Alfredo, and Dwight Taylor returned to Amaquería. They spent several days with scuba gear walking back and forth across the river bottom. To date, no one has ever found a single piece of the lost plane.

God had a better plan, though. Insurance payments plus funds raised by the Quiet Hour radio program made it possible to order a Cessna 180. The mission christened the new plane, equipped with a Robertson STOL conversion for use on short runways, the *Fernando Stahl II*—the *Fernando Stahl* flew again.

CHAPTER ELEVEN

GOD WILL PROVIDE!

Loving people, Clyde longed to take the gospel to every tribe, yet he had to fight a strong negative reaction toward the Chayawitas tribe, among the poorest of Indians in the Peruvian Amazon. Because they wore no clothing and roamed the jungle almost like animals, they had gained a reputation as dirty and ignorant.

Mission president Charles Case became interested in reaching this nomadic tribe of nearly 10,000 and presented the challenge to his staff. A lay preacher, Augusto Doñez, working as a carpenter at mission headquarters, spoke to Case about the possibility of witnessing to the unreached people. "You can find another carpenter," he said. "I'm volunteering to go as a missionary to the Chayawitas."

The Doñez family moved to Panáan and built a house on a bend of the Paranapura River. Augusto not only knew his Bible foreword and backward, he lived it. His family loved Jesus and the people they had come to serve. They treated the Chayawitas as brothers and sisters. Soon a Chayawita family built a thatched hut across the river. Then another and another. Finally a Chayawita family erected their home on the Doñez side of the river and started wearing clothing. Doñez taught them how to plant *yuca*, pineapple, rice, peanuts, mangos, and papaya. He believed that in order for the tribe to progress, they would need to learn the language of their country, so he started a school in which the native children learned to read the Bible in Spanish.

"Jesus is the Creator of the world and all the marvelous

things found in the jungle," he preached. "He died on the cross to save us from sin. Our Saviour is the best friend you can ever have. Soon Jesus is coming back to take those who love and serve Him to heaven."

He explained that one-tenth of all crops belonged to God and people should return them to Him as tithe. "God will open the windows of heaven and bless you," he said. "Besides tithe, you will want to bring special offering as gifts for God's work." The people brought produce for offerings at Sabbath school and church. The mission sold or traded the food and used the money to advance God's work.

Doñez led the Chayawitas in building one of the most attractive churches to be found at any Amazon mission station. It received no outside donations. The believers constructed everything, including the thatched steeple, from native materials found growing in the jungle.

The Doñez family kept loving the people and within four years the church grew to more than 300 members. New groups formed deeper in the jungle. The Chayawita village at Panáan became one of the most prosperous Indian villages in the Upper Amazon. Its people built a runway and the new *Fernando Stahl* and the *Ricardo Hayden* began making regular visits.

Clyde Peters planned to spent one weekend at Panáan. During Sabbath dinner at the Doñez home, Augusto asked, "Could you fly me to Balsa Puerto this afternoon. It's 15 minutes by air. A group of Chayawitas living near this jungle trade center want to learn how to observe the Sabbath."

Taking a translator, they flew out in the super cub, *Ricardo Hayden,* with its oversized tires for landing on rough strips. "They built a landing field several years ago," Augusto said, "but no plane has ever landed on it."

Clyde circled the village. Grass covered what appeared to be the airstrip. "How tall is the grass?" he asked.

"I don't know, but we really need to see these people."

"I really shouldn't land here, Augusto. You better hang on because it may be rough. I'll come in slowly, and with our big tires we should make it."

The tiny airplane nearly sank out of sight in grass standing from three to six feet tall. "Augusto," Clyde frowned, "how do you think we will ever get out of here?"

The town was having a big fiesta—all the adults were drunk.

People ran out through the high grass and some began banging on the plane. "Disgusting," Clyde muttered when he noticed a couple people pushing sticks through the airplane fabric.

"Please move back from the plane," Augusto pled.

The people refused to budge. "Who are you to tell us what to do?"

"These people are rude," Peters said. "We made a big mistake landing here."

Little by little, the people returned to the village and continued drinking and dancing. "We've got to find this Chayawita family," Augusto said as they left the plane. "I think they live on the edge of town."

The two men and their translator walked down the main street, trying not to bump into the pigs and cows that wandered freely about. "Watch where you're going, Clyde, if you want to avoid stepping into fresh manure," Augusto warned.

They kept asking for the family Augusto wanted to visit. "We don't know where they live," someone said, "but we just saw them in a bar."

At the nearby bar a man told them, "No, they're not here. There's another bar on the other side of town."

"What kind of people are we looking for anyway?" Clyde questioned. "They want to learn about the Sabbath, yet they're in a bar on Sabbath afternoon?"

At the other bar, they asked again. "No, they're not here. We haven't seen them for months."

Out in the filthy street, they met a drunk Indian who said he knew the family. "You will have to cross the river. Turn to the right and walk up river for half an hour. You'll find their hut."

"I bet it's at least an hour," Peters muttered. "They always make it sound closer than it really is."

"You're probably right. It's getting late and we better get going."

"Augusto, we haven't drunk any water and I feel hungry."

"If we're going to find these people before dark, you'll have to wait."

"Augusto, what's going to happen to the airplane?"

The sun was almost down when they arrived at the thatched hut more than an hour after starting to walk up the river. Inside, a group of people sat on the floor in a circle. "We know that today is the Sabbath, but we don't know how to worship," they told the visitors through the translator.

All of a sudden it hit home for Clyde. *These people weren't in a bar as they told us. They haven't been near one for months. The Holy Spirit's been working, and they really do want to know how to love Jesus and worship on His holy day.*

Augusto stood with his Bible and explained that "the great God of heaven created our world in six days. He rested on the seventh. He blessed it. He made it holy." The people listened eagerly to every word. When Augusto finished his sermon long after sundown, the people promised to meet and worship every Sabbath.

These people are so eager, Clyde thought. *My own religion is like filthy rags compared to these simple Chayawitas. They're really eager to follow Christ and do His will.*

Three hours after sundown they told their new friends goodbye and started back along the river to town. "Augusto," Clyde asked, "where are we going to eat? I'm starved! There are no restaurants in the town and everything is filthy. I'm too weak to walk much further."

"Don't worry about starving, Clyde," the lay preacher countered, "God will provide!"

As they tried to avoid stumbling over the pigs wallowing in the dark streets, a small boy called from the blackness, "*Señores,* come with me." He led them down an alley to another street and knocked on a door. The only sober adult in town lived in the rustic thatched house. A woman opened the door and invited them in. Clyde felt his stomach growling as he admired the simple home. *Everything is neat and clean!*

"You must be hungry," the woman said, leading them into another room.

Clyde looked in wonder, *A white table cloth! Knives, forks, spoons! Real china! All of this out here in the jungle?* The woman served soup, bread, rice, *yuca,* bananas, papaya—all the wonderful things that grow in the Amazon. *Only my wife, Eleanor, could have prepared a better meal than this,* he thought. *I've been grumbling about not having food, yet we've been invited to a banquet.*

"The government sent me here as the only school teacher in town," the middle-aged woman explained. "I'm sorry for the way the people are acting. Every time they have a fiesta, people start drinking and loose all control."

While still eating, they heard a loud knock on the door. It was the chief of police, obviously intoxicated, but still able to communicate. "My wife's very sick," he said. "She stepped on a bone a couple of weeks ago and her foot's infected. The local first aid station gave her penicillin injections, but her foot just gets worse."

"We will go and take a look," Augusto promised.

On the way Clyde asked, "Where are we going to sleep tonight? The teacher didn't have a room. I haven't seen any hotels."

Augusto, trusting God to work something out, avoided the question. They arrived at the house and the chief of police took them to his wife's room. With her hair pushed straight up, she sat on her bed under a mosquito net, moaning softly as she held her leg.

Because of the intense pain, the woman hadn't slept for days. In the dim light of a kerosene lamp her foot looked terrible. Augusto poked Clyde, "Let's go outside." Before leaving, though, they assured the woman that they would be back.

Out in the street, the men bowed their heads as Augusto prayed. "Lord, this is too much for us. We need Your help. Give us wisdom to do the right thing to help this suffering woman."

After praying, they returned to the house. Augusto asked for hot water and ice. Clyde eyed him. "Where in Balsa Puerta do you think we can find ice?"

They sent a boy to the teacher's house. She owned a small kerosene refrigerator—the only one in town. The boy brought back all the ice she had.

Augusto began the treatment by putting the infected foot in hot water for five or six minutes. The woman screamed when they put her foot in the ice water. The men alternated hot and cold for 45 minutes. The infected sore on the bottom of the woman's foot opened up and yellow pus began to drain out. The woman said to her husband, "This is the first relief I've had in days." Soon she fell asleep.

It was after midnight when they started to leave. "Send someone to get us in a couple of hours," Augusto told the woman's husband, "and we'll give your wife another treatment," then added, "I'm not sure where you can find us because we don't have a place to stay."

The police chief, though still not exactly sober, began to make more sense. "Oh," he said, "I've got a place for you to stay." He took them to police headquarters, ordered the men on duty to leave, and gave them beds with clean sheets.

"Augusto!" Clyde marveled. "I worried about a place to sleep and here we are with the best beds in town. God does provide!"

The exhausted men slept soundly. Two hours later, the boy stood outside. "*Capitáan! Doctor!* It's time for the *Señora* to have another treatment." The men stumbled through the dark grimy street and found the woman still sleeping. They gave her another hydrotherapy treatment and said, "Wait two hours and send someone to summon us again."

At 5:00 a. m. the boy arrived once more and they gave a third hot and cold water treatment. When they finished, Clyde and Augusto went back to the teacher's home for a delicious breakfast. Around 8:00 o'clock they returned for one final hydrotherapy session. The police chief, perfectly sober, thanked them again and again for what they had done for his wife.

"I'm sending 150 men to cut the grass on the airstrip," he said. Clyde spent the rest of the day pulling teeth while Augusto visited with the people. Late that afternoon they went out to the airstrip— all the tall grass had been macheted, leaving a smooth runway. Almost everyone came to watch them fly away. Augusto asked them to bow their heads while he prayed for the whole town.

The police chief embraced the men, saying, "After sleeping all morning, my wife got up for the first time in days. She washed and combed her hair. Her pain is gone. Thank you for all you've done."

People crowded close, but no one touched the plane. "Please come back and start a church for us," they pled.

Two weary men and their translator climbed into the plane for the short flight back to Panáan. "I've never seen anything like this," Clyde said to Augusto. "The whole town made a 180° turn in less than 24 hours. Our air ministry wouldn't be worth much if it weren't for Spirit-filled Peruvian workers like you. I see why God's work in Panáan has grown so fast."

Augusto Doñez, seeing a tremendous change in Clyde's attitude from the day before smiled, "Just thank the Lord!"

"When we walked up the river," Clyde continued, "I expected to find a bunch of drunk Chayawitas. Instead, we found a sober group sitting in a circle eager to learn how to worship the God of heaven. I worried about my stomach and a place to sleep, but God took care of everything. You're right Augusto. God does provide!"

TWELVE-GAUGE SHOTGUN

A nother Chayawita family roamed the jungle up river from Panán. The father, though knowing nothing about Jesus or the Bible, learned about the mission school from Chayawita friends who visited the mission station at Panán. "This is what I want for our boy." he told his wife. "I want him to go to school."

The non-Christian father waited for an opportunity to talk with his son. "I want to take you to the mission school. They will teach you to read and write." The father didn't know anything about reading and writing, but he thought it would be a good thing for his son to get an education.

"But Dad," the boy objected, "I don't want to go to school. I have a blowgun and you taught me how to make my own bow and arrows. I can hunt. I don't need school!"

Several weeks later word reached the Chayawita family that a big camp meeting would convene at Panán. The father went to his son. "Marco, let's go out in the jungle and build a new canoe."

The boy knew their old canoe was in bad shape. *Here's my chance to learn how to construct a canoe,* he thought. *Someday I'll make one on my own.*

"When we finish the canoe," his father continued, "we can take it down the river and visit the camp meeting."

The boy balked. "No! No! No!"

The father tried another tactic. "When we finish the canoe, we'll go hunting and kill a deer. Then we'll take it down the river to Panán and have a big feast." The stubborn boy insisted that he was not interested.

The patient father didn't give up. He owned what few Chayawitas had ever put their hands on. Several years before he had traded some jungle relics for an old beat-up single-barreled 12-gauge shotgun. "Marco," he said, "We'll build the canoe, go hunting, and then travel down the river. While we hunt, you can carry the gun. When we find the deer, I'll let you shoot."

The boys eyes lit up. "I'd like that. I've been hoping you'd let me use your gun."

Father and son walked back into the jungle and found a tall, straight mahogany tree. It stood near a stream where they could float a canoe. Together, they worked at cutting the tree until it crashed to the ground. All the time they worked on the canoe, the boy thought about just one thing. He kept reminding his father, "You're going to let me shoot the gun." Carefully they hollowed out the tree trunk, completing a solid mahogany canoe in only a few days. It was smooth and straight, as if it had come right out of a factory. The skilled father, with his son, did all the work using only primitive tools.

Chayawita Indians know how to hunt a wild animal. Natives employ the same kind of skill to stalk an animal that a cat uses to catch a mouse. To kill a large animal with a blow-gun or a bow and arrow, it's necessary to get very close. And to shoot a deer with an old beat-up shotgun it's also important to be as close as possible.

The father had only one shell. "Son," he said, "you have just one chance to kill the deer."

"I hear you, Father," the boy responded.

"This dangerous weapon will blow apart when it's fired unless you follow my instructions. In order to pull the trigger with your right hand, you must hold the gun together with your left. You must be very careful to get almost on top of the deer before shooting."

Leaving before sunrise, he handed his son the loaded gun. Barefoot, wearing only G-strings, father and son walked into the rain forest. Almost immediately they began tracking a deer, patiently stalking it all morning.

For a while they became separated, and when they found each other again, Marco's father signaled he was going back. "*No, I want to shoot this shotgun. I'm not stopping until I get my deer,*" Marco thought.

He kept going until he saw the movement of the deer straight ahead. The sights on the gun had broken off so he just looked down the barrel. Holding the gun together, he pulled the trigger. *Bang!* He thought the gun was blowing up, but he heard his prey fall. After racing through the underbrush, he pushed away the leaves hiding what he had shot. A deer? No. A direct hit? Yes! On the ground lay his father, his face full of buckshot.

The boy knelt beside his motionless father and looked at all the blood. What could he do? His people might be primitive, their hair scraggly and only a G-string for clothing, but they have hearts and care deeply for family members. Heartsick, the son desperately questioned, *How did I do this?* Rushing to the river, he returned with a handful of water. Too late—nothing could help. His father was dead.

Night came. The teenager picked up the shotgun and began the long, terrible journey, transporting his father's body through the darkness back to the camp where father and son had made the canoe.

Around midnight, Marco looked high in the sky. Directly overhead were four bright stars—the Southern Cross. He didn't know anything about the significance of the cross, and it brought him no comfort. After pushing the new canoe into the water, he then strained to place his father's stiff body into the bottom of the dugout. Exhausted and grief-stricken, the perplexed youth asked himself, *What shall I do now? Shall I paddle upstream to find my mother?*

Something inside his head kept saying, *Panán, Panán, Panán! My father wanted to take me to the mission at Panán!* He shoved the canoe into the river. *It's easier to go downstream. It's tough paddling upstream against the current.* As he drifted downstream he could not imagine where his journey would lead him.

The boy paddled and drifted all night, all the next day, and all the following night. The canoe, carrying a decaying corpse, arrived midmorning at Panán where the jungle camp meeting was in progress. An Indian saw the boy with a dead body and ran ahead to alert Augusto Doñez. Interrupting the meeting, Augusto announced that someone had died. Everyone got up and ran to the river. Clyde, also present, followed the crowd to the river.

The father, dead for two days, looked terrible. The boy appeared half dead himself. His eyes were red and bloodshot. Weeping all the way down the river, he had slept little. "This kid's no good," Clyde told Augusto when he learned the boy had shot his father in the face. "They probably had a fight. The boy got drunk and killed his dad."

Clyde watched Christian Chayawitas carefully, almost lovingly, pick up the father's naked body. Others hurried to start digging a grave. Augusto got his saw and cut boards to fit the top of the canoe. Kind hands wrapped the body with cloth and gently placed it back in the bottom of the canoe. Clyde marveled as Augusto nailed boards to the top of the canoe, turning it into a casket. They carried it to the freshly dug grave and held a graveside service.

Augusto took the boy to his home, gave him clothes, and fed him boiled yucca. Marco slept fitfully, haunted by the terrible thing he had done.

Each day Augusto set aside a specific time to spend with the boy. Clyde listened when the lay preacher started talking to Marco through a translator. "There is a God in heaven who knows about you and loves you. He knows all about your dad. He's preparing a home for us in heaven. He's going to come back and take us to be with Him."

The boy sat there, stone-faced, shutting out the world. "You're wasting your time," Clyde said. "This kid isn't worth all your effort to help him. You can see he's not interested in a word you're saying."

Augusto smiled and went right on speaking to the boy. "You know," he looked at Marco, "I believe you are going to see your father again."

Marco's eyes jerked open wide and he listened to every word. He sat up like a college student studying for a final exam. "Do you mean I'll be able to tell my father I didn't mean to shoot him?" he asked.

"When Jesus comes back He will call those who serve God. They'll rise up out of their graves—we will see our families again." At that the young man began to weep. He wanted to hear more and more.

The boy went to all the meetings and studied the Bible with Augusto every day. He learned that Jesus forgives sin, even that of a young man who had killed his father. Clyde watched as the Holy Spirit worked overtime, speaking in the Chayawita language to a young Indian boy.

Marco began to understand how God had used the tragic death of his father to bring him to the mission station. He began to believe that the death of God's Son on the cross of Calvary made it possible for him to have eternal life.

On the final Sabbath of camp meeting 78 people were baptized. Marco, the boy who had killed his father with a 12-gauge shotgun, was baptized in the name of the Father, the Son, and the Holy Spirit. Still skeptical, Clyde questioned, "Does this kid really know enough to be baptized?"

One thing was for sure—the boy's character, the expression on his face, his actions had all changed. He was a new person. No longer naked, he wore clothes. More than that, he accepted the robe of Christ's righteousness. Christ's righteousness is for Chayawitas too. Marco's canoe had been buried with his father, his sins in the river with Jesus.

The day after the baptism, Chayawita Adventists gave Marco another canoe. He couldn't wait to make the long trip up the river to find his family and tell them the news of the resurrection and the soon coming of Jesus.

It's hard to paddle up a river and it takes courage for a Chayawita to live for Christ. But Marco loved Jesus and with His help determined to love God and keep His commandments. He couldn't read or write, but he took a Bible with him. He wanted to show his people the Word of God. As a result of his witness, a new Chayawita village formed. They built an airstrip and started a church.

Will Marco's father be in heaven? Only God knows for sure. The father probably didn't even know about Jesus, but he lived up to the light he had. He did everything he could to get Marco to go to Panán. His death brought his son to the Adventist camp meeting and a knowledge of Jesus' love.

CHAPTER THIRTEEN

AFTER THE PARACHUTE OPENED

Years later Clyde had spent Christmas Eve in bed with hepatitis, facing a slow recovery. The next morning, learning that an airliner with 92 people on board had vanished, he had climbed out of bed and joined a massive search.

Seventeen-year-old Juliane, a survivor of the crash, walked out of the jungle 11 days later. The information she provided enabled the search teams to locate the crash sight the next morning. On the twelveth day Clyde had volunteered to parachute into the Amazon jungle in an effort to find more survivors.

Skydivers feel relief when their parachute opens. But for Clyde it brought him his greatest grief. He had jumped out of the helicopter, counted to five, and pulled the ripcord on his parachute. Unfortunately the knot he had hastily tied to secure the chain saw he would need to clear a landing site for the helicopter now failed. The vital chain saw dropped away, crashing into the jungle below.

"Dear Lord," Clyde prayed after the parachute opened, "without the saw, I can never clear a place for helicopters to land. Without the compass I left in the plane, I'll soon be lost. You know the mess I'm in, Lord, I need Your help."

He worried about his plan to land at the crash site. "Lord, if I hit wreckage the wrong way, I may be injured or even kill myself. All I can do is find a nice 'fluffy' tree." Adjusting the lines on his chute, he headed for a tall one. "I'm going to land here. It looks just like cotton." In his heart he knew better.

A parachute with 746 square feet of rip-stop nylon has to catch on something, Clyde figured. But instead, as it fell through the tree branches, the parachute collapsed and he dropped like a bullet. *Man! Falling this fast I'll break my neck!*

Pulling his feet and knees together, he put his arms over his face. Tree limbs ripped off his watch. Suddenly Clyde hung in his harness 15 feet above the ground. "Dear Lord, You've saved my life. The way my parachute caught in a small tree under a tall one is absolutely perfect. In 800 jumps, this is the softest landing I've ever had, but how do I get to the ground?"

Glancing around, he saw a tree trunk 28 inches in diameter just two feet in front of him. "You've solved another problem, Lord. There's no thorns or poisonous ants on it." With one hand he unhooked his capwells, then wrapped both arms and legs around the tree and slid to the ground.

"Loving Lord," Clyde prayed, "this is unfriendly territory. I don't have a chain saw, not even a machete. You got me out of the tree, and if I ever escape this jungle it will be because of Your help." He fired a flare to let the helicopter crew know he was OK.

Now that he was on the ground, Peters shouted in every direction, hoping to hear a reply from some survivor waiting for help. Next he pulled out a 357 Magnum and fired several shots. The gun makes a lot of noise and if anything would attract people, it surely would. Although he didn't exactly expect people to come running, he felt sure there had to be survivors. *I can't be more than 1,500 feet from the crash site*, he calculated. *I'll find anyone who's still alive!*

Standing still, he listened. *I hear someone groaning!* Dropping his equipment, he ran in the direction of the sound. The stench of rotting human flesh filled the air. As he went he kept looking back to make sure he wouldn't get lost.

I've been fooled, he realized on reaching the source of the sound. *The groaning comes from a tiny stream flowing over a piece of metal from the wrecked plane.*

A United States Air Force Hercules C-130 circled 8,000 feet over his head. Peters watched buzzards land and fly away. Airplanes flew in all directions, their pilots expecting a signal from Clyde. The first flare would let them know he was OK. After that, a red flare if all were dead and a white flare if he found survivors. Since he had already fired the first flare, he thought to himself, *I'd better not fire any more until I find survivors.*

The shock over losing the chain saw worked on his troubled mind. *How long can I survive? I don't even have a compass.*

Clyde headed back to pick up his equipment. *It'll be easy to find the parachute I left hanging in a tree,* he assured himself. He found the tree, but no parachute. *Wait a minute, I must be confused. This isn't the tree!*

Although he kept searching, he failed to locate the parachute or his equipment. *I'm totally lost!* The truth hit hard. *Oh, well—I'll keep looking for survivors. That's why I'm here.*

The helicopter he had jumped from kept flying back over. Clyde tried to follow it. First he thought it was over the accident site, then decided it must be looking for him. The more he chased it, the more disoriented he became. The helicopter crew hadn't seen the flare Clyde fired, nor did they notice any trees being cut down. They guessed he had met with disaster and the report went out that he was dead.

I'm completely drained, Clyde told himself. *All my food's with the equipment under the tree where my parachute hangs. All I have now is this Magnum 357, a hunting knife, and my small day pack.* The buckle holding the top of the knife sheaf kept coming unsnapped so he checked it frequently to make sure the knife was still there.

The gun he had brought to Peru himself, then sold it. Its new owner had handed it to him as he boarded the helicopter. "Take my gun, you may need it." He reached for the knife to cut away some jungle undergrowth—it was gone.

Clyde estimated he had tramped 10 miles on the jungle floor without finding the crash site. The only evidence of an air disaster was the constant smell of death. He drank water from tiny jungle streams, then worried they might be contaminated with rotting human bodies.

He carried no raincoat, not even a piece of plastic. At sundown, it began to rain hard. As he tried to build a shelter, without either a machete or knife, it proved difficult. Tearing off a few large jungle leaves provided some protection. By morning he lay in a pool of mud. But he didn't need to wake up—he'd never gone to sleep.

During the long wet night, he took stock of his own life. He wanted to be right with God and prayed, "Lord, give me more faith." Thoughts of Jesus brought encouragement. "Even in my weakened condition, Lord, I know You will take care of me." Somehow he felt a sense of assurance. "If it's Your will, please lead me to the crash site." From the moment Clyde first learned of the LANSA accident, he had kept asking himself, *How would I feel if my children were on that plane?*

By 4:30 in the morning, the rain slowed to a drizzle. Clyde stood up in the mud. *Time for morning worship. Wish I had a good devotional book. At least I can repeat Bible promises.* His voice echoed through the jungle as he sang. After praying, he resumed his search, trudging around looking for survivors.

Later in the morning the rain clouds vanished and helicopters and airplanes began combing the area again. Looking up through the tall trees, Clyde watched them circle overhead. *They're probably looking for me. But unless I locate the crash site or find a clearing, there's no way they'll ever see me. I doubt they spotted the flare I fired after landing yesterday. It probably never cleared the treetops.*

When he fired another, hoping to attract attention, it apparently didn't reach above the trees either. Next he fired a white flare—it fizzled. At an open area where several trees had fallen, he climbed up on a tree trunk and reasoned, *Maybe the best thing I can do is just sit here.* At least the sunshine dried his wet clothes.

Since his only food consisted of one small bag of peanuts, he decided to ration them. *It's been 13 days since I learned about the LANSA crash and got out of bed, still suffering with hepatitis. Each day my strength has increased as I searched for the missing plane. What will happen to me now without food?*

Having hiked around the jungle the day before, spent a sleepless night, and had only a few peanuts for breakfast, he thought to himself, *I better conserve my energy. This is no time for a hepatitis relapse!*

About an hour later a helicopter passed overhead, then flew away without seeing him. He wondered why it kept coming back. *I could sit here for the rest of my life and they'll never see me.* Ambling off in the direction of the chopper, he became disoriented. *Guess the best thing is to head back to where I was on the fallen tree.*

The hilly terrain made each step difficult. After an hour and a half he hardly had strength to climb the last little hill and perch himself on the tree trunk where he had been before. Perspiration and pushing through wet jungle undergrowth had soaked his clothing. *It's hopeless! My efforts are getting me nowhere and my strength's gone. I might as well give up.*

But after sitting for two hours watching the helicopter and airplanes, Clyde felt better. *I need to get moving and find the acci-*

dent site. He knew his wife Eleanor, his children, and many friends were praying for him. *If they're so faithful, the least I can do is forge ahead, find the crash site, and get out of here.*

His efforts to locate the crash became more confusing. Odors of dead flesh came from every direction, yet he didn't find any bodies. Suddenly, at the bottom of a creek in front of him, he saw two airplane engines. *I must be close to the main part of the plane,* he conjectured. But when he walked into the jungle at different angles from the engines, he found absolutely nothing.

Late in the afternoon it started raining hard as he crawled up a river bank. More discouraged than ever, he removed his harness, day pack, and pistol, and laid them down under a tree. He looked around. *This area is boxed in by the river so I'll find it again.*

Six hundred feet away he found a tree—freshly broken. *Only a crashing plane could break down a big tree like this,* he told himself. Although he searched in every direction, he discovered nothing. Worse, he couldn't find the tree where he had left the gun and day pack. Nor could he even locate the river.

How could I be so stupid? he asked himself. He felt responsible for the problems of the last couple days. *I lost the chain saw because I didn't tie it properly. I landed too far from the accident site. I left my equipment under the tree with the parachute and haven't been able to find it since. Then I lost my knife. Now I've lost the gun and day pack. I'm lost too. It'll soon get dark and I don't have a place to sleep.*

Totally disoriented, Peters stumbled along until he came to a clearing with a swamp. He waved frantically when a helicopter soared overhead but its crew didn't see him. Four times it returned, and each time he waved. *No hope,* Clyde decided, *I'm only a speck in this huge jungle. They'll never see me.*

Hungry and weak, he reached a small stream flowing out of the swamp and followed it. Before long, it grew to a fair-sized river. Around a bend, straight ahead on a sandbar, a 15-foot crocodile stretched out in the last rays of the late afternoon sun. Although it faced the other way, it's eyes were up and saw him. Whipping around, it shot toward him like a bullet. Clyde jumped up just in time to allow the crocodile to race under him. "Wow!" Standing breathless, he talked to God. "I left the gun under a tree. My machete went down with the chain saw. Now I jump up and it's as if I was hovering while the crocodile ran under me, straight to the river. Jesus, You took care of me. I didn't need a gun!"

Wearing a wet jumpsuit, wet socks, a wet pair of boots and wet leather gloves, Clyde had absolutely nothing to protect him except the Lord. Thirsty, he drank water from a clear stream flowing into the river.

"Thank You, Lord, for the water. You know I'm hungry and need food too. My physical condition isn't good—I can't afford a relapse of hepatitis."

Reaching down, he pulled up some grass roots—they tasted bitter and he spit them out. Then he tried another kind of grass with white roots that looked like spaghetti. They tasted delicious, almost like lettuce. Palm fronds grew nearby. He worked to tear them open without the aid of a knife. Inside he found delicious tasting palm hearts. "God, You're giving me the best food I could possibly have here in a wild jungle."

A stomach full of grass roots and palm hearts made him feel much better. "Lord, You do provide," he prayed. "I didn't have to shoot a deer or a bird for food. Nor did I have to kill a crocodile to stay alive."

Searching for a place to spend the night, he found the ideal spot for a bed underneath a tree on the river bank. Rain was falling again. Feeling the need to hurry, he quickly gathered leaves, some to go under him, some over him, and more for a pillow. Then he stacked 20 rocks near the leaf pillow thinking, *If this spot turns out to be the home of a crocodile, I'll be prepared. I'll keep a big stick here, too.*

Clyde lay down in his bed with layers of leaves both under and over him, then put his wet jumpsuit on top of the leaves to help hold them in place. For the first time since jumping into the jungle he felt reasonably comfortable. From his cozy bed he watched bolts of lightning fill the Amazon sky. Rolling peals of ground-shaking thunder rumbled through the jungle, followed by torrential rain.

When it quieted down, he heard a strange sound only a few feet away. A crocodile arrived, wanting to claim its bed. Clyde threw a rock and heard the large reptile hit the water in the river below. Unwilling to be deprived of its bed, the persistent crocodile kept returning. Each time Peters threw a rock, he lost more leaves, until all the leaves he had for blankets were gone and he shivered in the cold. Getting back into his wet jumpsuit did not provide the warmth he needed. Mosquitos and other insects attacked him, making it the worst night of his life.

Clyde mulled the situation over in his restless mind. *I got myself into this mess—there's no way out. If I just had a large piece of plastic, I'd stay dry. Right now I'd gladly give $100 for a piece of plastic. If only a jungle Indian would come by, he'd help me build a shelter.*

His bed in the crocodile haunt turned into a mud hole. When dawn broke, Clyde struggled to his feet. *I'm more of a mud man than a human being.* Lacking soap, razor, and toothbrush, he walked into the river to clean up. As he moved around in the water, now warmer than the air, his chilled body began to warm up.

Oh, it's morning worship time. It won't be fancy. He sang and quoted more Bible promises, then prayed. "Thank You, Father, for getting me through a miserable night. And, Lord, I know You are going to give me a good breakfast. I already feel much better after eating the grass roots and palm hearts last night."

He struggled to make a decision. "Shall I sit here until a ground crew arrives?" Clyde asked the Lord. "Or should I follow the river?"

Two days of searching had produced no evidence of survivors. He rolled several logs into the river thinking he might use one to float down stream. All were waterlogged and sank. "Lord, I need to know what to do," he pled. "There are no balsa trees around here, and even if there were, it's impossible to build a raft without a machete or any other tool."

Spotting a good-sized log, he said, "I'll roll it into the river, Lord. If it sinks, I'll stay here and pray for ground crews to arrive soon. If it floats, I'll ride it down the river."

After splashing into the water, the log floated. "I believe this is Your answer, Lord. I'm going down the river." He crawled across the log and sat on it. It held him up although he sat in water. After finding a smaller log, he used jungle vines to tie it crosswise, hoping to make his log craft more stable. Using a stick for a paddle, he straddled the log and pushed out into the current. Every few hundred feet he fell off and struggled to get back on. After a mile or more, he learned to navigate without falling off so frequently. Paddling with a round stick became difficult when the river backed up into a swamp. He considered walking, but decided against it.

When he discovered the swamp had formed from flood waters pouring in from the Shebonya river, he paddled extra hard, reaching the main river where the current picked him up and sent him speeding down stream. *If I can keep this up,* he thought, *I'll reach the woodcutters hut where Juliane stayed and get help.*

New dangers lay ahead in a river filled with log jams and floating debris, though. He received bruises every time he banged into something. Rounding a river bend, a whirlpool spun him around, then threw him down the river to fight more rapids.

The nose of his log "canoe" rose about a foot out of the river, but Clyde actually sat waist deep in water. After traveling five hours, and falling off at least 15 times, he shivered and shook so much from the cold that he decided to pull to shore and let the sun warm him up.

Dry and warm, after soaking up the sun, he straddled his log to continue on down river. Now in a current still swift, but with fewer rapids and less debris, he made better time. By 2:00 in the afternoon a noise in the distance caught his attention. He listened carefully, *I hear a motor!* "Thank you, Lord. What a beautiful sight," he exclaimed as a boat appeared around the bend. "This is what I've prayed for!"

Men came along side and helped him climb aboard their boat. "You must be a survivor from the LANSA accident," they said.

"No, I'm Clyde Peters."

"Oh, we heard you disappeared after jumping into the jungle to search for survivors. They reported you were dead. Sure glad we found you!"

Late that afternoon an airplane flew low over the river. Sighting a boat, the pilot, Jerrie Cobb, world famous woman aviator accompanied by Robert Hummerstone from *Life* magazine, circled and dropped even lower to get a good view. Unknown to Clyde, his wife Eleanor was in the plane, her eyes fixed on him. "That's my husband in the boat!" she exclaimed. "God has answered our prayers!"

The sun slipped low behind the tall jungle trees as the boat carrying Clyde arrived at the mouth of the Shebonya river and started up the Pachitea toward Puerto Inca. They met a speed boat looking for Clyde, and he transferred to the faster boat. As it grew dark, the operator strained his eyes to dodge the logs and debris floating on the swollen river. Reaching Puerto Inca late in the evening, Clyde enjoyed a good meal and his first real sleep since parachuting into the crash area.

Before the sun had popped out over the jungle in the morning, he climbed into the *Fernando Stahl II* and flew to the air base at Yarina Cocha. "You're home! You're home!" his excited wife and children greeted him. After a shower and breakfast, he took student missionary Dan Wenberg and flew back to Puerto Inca.

Ground crews had reached the LANSA wreckage and cleared trees. Clyde and Dan were invited to take a helicopter flight to the crash site. When the chopper touched down on the newly prepared pad, Clyde opened the door and sniffed. "This is the same ugly stench I smelled for three days after my jump into the jungle."

Broken pieces of fuselage along with other parts of the airplane stretched out over a large area. Clyde looked in silence at the accident scene. Christmas gifts from broken suitcases lay scattered over the ground. Little dolls wrapped in bright paper, model airplanes, cars, all kinds of toys and other gifts littered the jungle floor—gifts for younger brothers and sisters and parents, gifts that would never be delivered.

The wrecked airplane had been filled with youth, teenagers who had just finished another year in school. Young people who anticipated enjoying the holidays with their families. Full of life and enthusiasm, they had looked forward to a bright future. No one dreamed it would be their last flight. Ninety-one died. Only Juliane had lived.

Before leaving home that morning, Clyde's neighbor, Floyd Lyons, gave him a description of his son's clothing. The boy had been on the plane. Many bodies had been retrieved, but not Nathan's. "Dear Lord," Clyde prayed, "please help me find Nathan's remains."

Even now, with well marked trails and much of the jungle undergrowth cut away, it was still easy to get lost. He took his compass and followed a heading for a mile into the jungle. Nothing. Returning, he tried another heading. Again nothing. Once more he retraced his steps to the wreckage and walked a mile out in a different direction. Finally he stopped, ready to give up.

"Wait!" Right in front of him was a body, mostly bones.

He called Dan Wenberg. "This is a miracle!" Peters stood staring at a skeleton covered with shreds of clothing. "The clothing's exactly what Nathan Lyons wore on the doomed flight. The Lord led us to this spot."

His heart ached for his grieving neighbors who longed for their son to be found. Clyde took a black plastic body bag and carefully picked up what remained of the 14-year-old boy. "I'm glad Jesus knows how to breathe life into these bones and make them live again," he said.

Fighting tears and nausea, Clyde and Dan picked up 11 more decomposed bodies and stuffed them into body bags. Before leaving the crash site, they searched for the gear Clyde had lost after parachuting into the jungle. They found nothing, so he made plans to buy a new chain saw for its owner and a Magnum 357 for the man who had loaned him the gun.

The helicopter flew them back to Puerto Inca. Peters transferred the bag containing what was left of Nathan Lyons to the mission plane and flew straight to the Linguistic air base. He choked up as he presented the boy's remains to his father and mother. "I'm sorry it has to be this way," he said.

The heartbroken parents thanked Clyde. "We're grateful for the help of the Seventh-day Adventist Mission in these difficult moments. It's a big relief to know our son's been found. At least we can plan a proper funeral now."

"I prayed for more survivors," Clyde said, "but it hasn't worked that way. My heart aches for all who lost children in this tragic airline crash." Yet he found encouragement knowing the day is coming when Jesus "will send his angels with a great sound of a trumpet, and they will gather together His elect . . . from one end of heaven to the other"(Matt. 24:31, NKJV).

On his next flight to Puerto Inca he picked up two Federal Aviation Agency inspectors. The men had just found the black box, a voice recorder located in the vertical fin of the plane's tail section and connected to a microphone in the cockpit. From the minute the master switch goes on and the pilot starts the engines, it records everything.

The black box recorder detailed the final moments of the Christmas Eve crash of LANSA Flight 508. The plane had carried plenty of fuel to fly to Iquitos or simply to circle until the storm passed. Instead, conversation in the cabin revealed a captain who refused to listen to his copilot and fly around the storm. He and his crew—joking, laughing, and making vulgar remarks—did not live to carry out their plans for a wild party on their return to Lima.

Later Clyde Peters shared his experience many times in churches and schools. "When I think of all who died, I understand why Jesus says, 'Be ready!' and not just 'Get ready!'

"My jump to find survivors failed. I lost the chain saw, the machete—all my equipment. I wandered in circles without finding a single survivor. In spite of such problems, it renewed my faith by forcing me to look at my own spiritual condition. I need constant communion with my Saviour. I've made a lot of resolutions and pray that Jesus will help me follow through on them.

"I pray that Jesus will always be the chief pilot in my life and lead me to do His will. Whether it's to fly a plane, dig a ditch, write a letter, make a missionary contact, give a Bible study, work as a farmer, or to just live a Christian life, I want to do my best with God's help.

"When I was out there picking up bones and broken skulls, I realized how fragile life is. I could have died parachuting into the jungle. But Jesus gave me more opportunity to work to hasten His return."

CHAPTER FOURTEEN

LITTLE RED WAGON

I t's a sad day for us," Clyde told the Seamounts when they returned to the United States. "I'm really going to miss you, Bob, and Ellen too." The men's age difference was enough to be that of father and son, but they had worked together like brothers.

Back in the States, Bob Seamount told how God employed mission aviation to reach people in the jungles of Peru. Soon the General Conference began authorizing the use of planes in other parts of the world.

One day they asked Bob, "What is the most economical way to get two airplanes to missions in Africa?" He started figuring. "I can fly a plane to Africa for less than it costs to build a shipping crate, and that's only the beginning. Other expenses will include disassembly, freight to the port, ocean freight, and reassembly at the destination."

Commercial shipping company bids came to $10,000 per plane, and the process would take several months. Bob assured the General Conference officers that he could transport the planes to Africa for about $2,500 each. Church leaders liked the idea and asked him to find another experienced pilot to help him ferry the planes across the Atlantic.

Working his ham radio one sultry evening at the air base in Yarina Cocha, Clyde Peters connected with Bob Seamount in the states via phone patch. Before going off the air, Bob said, "By the way, Clyde, could you help me? I've been asked to take two planes to Africa. Will you fly one of them?"

"You've been listening, Eleanor," Clyde turned to his wife. "Will it be OK with you?"

Eleanor, with a gleam in her eyes, questioned, "Fly over the Atlantic?" She hesitated. "I suppose it's all right if you want to take the risk. At least, you'll be doing it for God."

Back on the radio, Clyde said, "I just got the green light from Eleanor. It's a deal. I'll be glad to fly one of the planes across the Atlantic to Africa."

The two men finalized plans, and church leaders in South America, welcoming the opportunity to help missions in Africa, approved the trip for Clyde. Since he didn't have a lot of baggage, he told his children, "This is a perfect chance to take some jungle animals to the States."

He flew to Lima with two monkeys, an ocelot, and a carton with ten baby snakes. Checking into a hotel, he fed the animals and fell asleep. About 1:00 in the morning his phone rang insistently. Finally he woke up enough to pick up the receiver. "*Señor* Peters," an urgent voice spoke, "your snakes are escaping!"

Clyde knocked a few things over trying to find the light switch. He looked in the snake carton. No snakes—not one! Opening the door of his room, Clyde saw three terrified hotel attendants holding a broom and dustpan tied to long handles. From 15 feet away they tried to sweep the baby snakes into the dustpan.

The ruckus started when one of the snakes crawled into another hotel guest's room.

Attendants cringed when Clyde reached down and picked up the harmless baby boa constrictors. After putting all 10 snakes back into the box, he taped it shut and made a couple of small holes so the tiny creatures could breathe but not escape. Early in the morning, Clyde and his menagerie boarded a flight for San Antonio, Texas.

Burning inside, he tried hard not to show his anger when U. S. Customs agents confiscated the ocelot, Timmy, a longtime family pet. Fortunately, they passed the monkeys and snakes. Bob met Clyde and immediately they went to work preparing for the flight to Africa.

Early on a Friday morning two new mission planes lifted slowly from a Florida airport and headed out over the Caribbean. Bob flew the Cessna 185 and Clyde piloted the Cessna 182. Each carried its pilot, 200 gallons of fuel, and about 500 pounds of gear, including a two-person inflatable life raft.

Clyde watched cotton candy clouds float over the blue Caribbean. "This is a gorgeous day," he chatted with Bob on the radio. "The air is really smooth." Looking down, he added, "There's a lot of water below us, but I do see an island here and there. What will it be like over the Atlantic with only water and no islands?"

The pilots tested their fuel systems by using a hand pump to keep the right wing tank full. On Friday afternoon, they landed at Port of Spain, Trinidad, and stayed with the Adventist pastor. The next morning they worshiped at church where it seemed as if all 800 members shook their hands when they arrived for Sabbath school and then another 800 times after the services. With 1,600 handshakes they couldn't have felt more welcome.

When the church members discovered the two men would cross the Atlantic to deliver mission planes to Africa, one man stood up at announcement time and stated, "I think we should declare a day of fasting and prayer on the day these brethren cross the ocean. How many are in favor?"

Eight hundred hands went up. Actually, 802 because Clyde and Bob raised their hands too. Clyde nudged the older pilot. "We are blessed to know 800 of our brothers and sisters will be praying for our Atlantic flight." He appreciated all the warmth and encouragement, but inside he felt a strange chill, emotions similar to those he had gone through on his first solo flight or his first jump with a parachute.

On Sunday they flew past Guyana, Suriname, and French Guiana, then down the coast of Brazil, landing at Belém near the mouth of the Amazon. In spite of bad weather and a forced landing at Fortaleza, they arrived in Recife, Brazil about 10:30 a.m. on Tuesday.

Immediately they began checking their engines to make sure everything was in perfect condition for an ocean crossing. Clyde radioed Eleanor at the air base in Peru. "Everything's fine. We're having a great trip and the airplanes are performing well." But the truth was that he didn't feel good at all. The unknowns of a flight across the Atlantic weighed heavily on his mind.

By mid afternoon they finished servicing the engines and filled the gas tanks to maximum capacity. Clyde looked at the planes and shook his head. With all the weight, the landing gear spread out and the tires appeared to be half flat. Both Cessnas sat back on their tail skid and the nose wheel didn't reach the ground.

Wanting to leave by sundown, they rushed into the airport office to file a flight plan. The officer looked at their documents. "Africa? Single engine planes are not allowed to cross the South Atlantic from Brazil!"

"Did you say no Atlantic crossing?" Clyde leaned forward. "Sir, these are new planes. We have top-of-the-line radio equipment, including VHF with all the en route frequencies. In addition, we're carrying life rafts in case of an emergency and have plenty of fuel."

The official called the chief commander for the Brazilian Air Force. "I have two men here with single engine planes. They say they've got to cross the Atlantic tonight."

He explained the situation. After a long conversation he turned to Clyde and Bob. "Sorry. We don't accept single engine flights over the Atlantic. Not from Brazil."

Clyde looked at Bob Seamont. "I'm already tired of flying. We spent 12 hours crossing the Caribbean, 10 hours to Belém, and another 10 to get to Recife. It will cost our missions in Africa a fortune if we fly back to the States, up over Greenland, then down across Spain and on to Africa. We don't have money for this."

"I know, Clyde," Bob said, "but we don't have a choice."

The official started closing the office. Leading the men out, he locked the doors him. "I'll see you tomorrow. You're not going anywhere tonight."

Our backs are really against the wall now! Clyde thought.

He leaned against the building and started to pray. "These planes are for Your work in Africa, Lord. You know our concerns about this trip, but You brought us this far. Please work out Your will for our flight."

Inside the office the phone started ringing. The aviation officer was already more than 100 feet away. "Sir, your phone is ringing," Clyde called after him.

"I'll take care of it tomorrow," he answered.

"It might be something important!"

The Brazilian turned and grudgingly walked back to the office. The phone kept ringing and ringing. Although he fumbled with a bunch of keys before he could open the door, the phone persisted. Slowly he headed to his desk and threw his keys across the top. Instead of reaching for the phone, he walked around the desk.

"Who would call after office hours and let the phone ring so long?" Clyde asked Bob. "The way this guy's fooling around it's going to stop ringing before he answers."

Finally the officer picked up the phone. "Yes, yes, they're still here. Do you want to talk to them?"

The man handed the phone to Peters. "This is the commander general for Brazil's air force. Why did you fellows fly to Brazil planning to cross the Atlantic?" the voice asked.

"We need to take two planes to our mission in Africa. We had no idea that Brazil has restrictions for crossing with single engine planes. If we'd known, we would have taken the northern route over Greenland."

"I don't know why I'm doing this, but I'm going to make an exception. Since you have two planes equipped with life rafts, both with VHF radio equipment and en route frequencies, I'm going to authorize your flight plan."

"Thank you, sir," Clyde breathed.

"Don't ever come here again in a single engine plane and think you can fly from Brazil to Africa. We won't allow it! Now let me talk to the officer."

Clyde walked to a corner where Seamont prayed. "Bob, the commander asked to talk with the flight officer."

They both listened as the Brazilian said, "Yes, OK, OK. It's a deal. OK!" and hung up. The official stamped and signed the flight plan documents and handed copies to the men. "Guess I won't see you tomorrow. Have a good flight!"

The two pilots walked toward their airplanes. Clyde poked Bob. "I saw you over there praying. I've been praying, too. To be truthful, I've been very concerned about making this flight."

"You're not alone," Seamont admitted. "My mind's filled with visions of everything that could go wrong over the Atlantic."

"What just happened gives me faith God will be with us," Clyde replied. "First they tell us we can't cross the Atlantic from Brazil. We pray and the commander for Brazil's air force calls back after business hours and lets the phone ring and ring and ring."

"God is surely good," Bob answered.

"It's a miracle as far as I'm concerned. No one ever lets a phone ring so long. The Holy Spirit had to work on that man's mind for him to do this. And the local officer here, he didn't want to go back to the office, but he did."

With new confidence, the Adventist missionary pilots climbed into their planes, cranked the engines, and lumbered down the runway. Heavily loaded with fuel, it took three hours to reach 8,000 feet elevation.

"Glad you're along, Clyde," Bob radioed later.

Clyde reached for his microphone, "I'm delighted to be with you, Bob. How's the Cessna 185 doing?"

"Great. The engine is performing its best. Look's like I will keep busy though, you know, using the hand pump to keep transferring fuel into the right wing tank."

"Yeah," Clyde came back on, "The pump is giving me plenty of exercise, but this Cessna 182 is running great. The smooth air tonight is marvelous."

After six hours of clear, smooth flying, Bob and Clyde entered clouds and started flying on instruments. They had flown side by side. Now they separated with Bob in the lead, 15 miles ahead. Both pilots worked to keep on the correct heading.

Clyde's eyes stayed glued to his compass. *Boy, we're right on the money.* He thought about the words of David: *"Your word is a lamp to my feet and a light to my path"(Ps.119:105, NKJV). Living for the Lord is just like flying. You've got to keep your heading. And if you ever get off course, you'd better let Jesus help you back on.*

Maintaining a heading in smooth clouds proved easy but after 12 hours they encountered thunderstorms that lasted for six solid hours. *I've never seen a storm like this*, Clyde thought. *The turbulence is awesome.*

Heavy rain pelted the planes. They'd been flying steadily at 8,000 feet. Now thermal updrafts and downdrafts tossed the tiny planes around like leaves. Clyde looked at his altimeter in disbelief—*18,000 feet?* Suddenly the engine stopped dead. The Cessna 182 has a carburetor with a paper filter. Heavy rain had plugged it with water. Clyde quickly pulled carburetor heat. To his relief, the engine came back to life.

Ten minutes later he glanced at the altimeter—*Only 4,000 feet?*

Another updraft caught the plane and lifted it to 14,000 feet. Six times the engine stopped. Each time adrenaline shot through his body. *I won't worry*, Clyde determined. *When Brazil's air force commander called the Recife airport after closing time and let the phone ring and ring—there can be no doubt that God ap-*

proved this flight. Life has its turbulence, but if we cling to Jesus, He will see us through.

The fuel injection system on the Cessna 185 allows air to enter from inside the engine avoiding filter problems. This saved Bob the emotional strain of having his engine quit every few minutes. Both pilots kept setting their compasses, trying to hold a steady heading, but rough air caused extreme difficulty. Lightning filled their headsets with crackling noise when they tried to talk to each other on the radio.

They'd been in the air 18 hours—the last six in an incredible tropical storm. When they at last flew out of the storm, the blue Atlantic spread out below. Bob Seamont, 30 miles ahead, could see the coast of West Africa. They were 35 miles off course and made the necessary correction.

Bob was landing when Clyde got him on the radio, "I've arranged with a ham radio operator in New York to make a phone patch to General Conference headquarters."

"Bob Seamount just landed in Africa," he reported to church leaders. "I'm on a three-mile final leg into Monrovia, Liberia. God has taken both planes safely across the Atlantic."

On the ground at last, Clyde crawled out of his plane. Bob sat there with the door of the 185 open. "In all my years of flying I've never been in weather like we just came through," Seamont said. They photographed both planes to record where the severe rain had chewed away the paint right down to bare metal on the leading edge of the wings, struts, spinner, and nose cowlings.

The tired men walked away with their suitcases, leaving their airplane doors wide open. Half way to a hotel, Clyde remembered them. Returning, they locked the planes. Clyde slumped down in the back seat of the taxi. "You know that statement, Bob: 'We have nothing to fear for the future except as we forget the way the Lord has led us in the past.' God took care of us today. We can sure trust Him tomorrow."

They learned that a Boeing 707 jet left Brazil about the same time they did and arrived two hours late in Dakar because of the severe storm. "I'm really thankful," Clyde said, "for the faith of the church members in Trinidad who spent the day of our flight in fasting and prayer."

"Yes. And while we were being tossed around for six hours in terrible turbulence, I kept thinking about the providential approval of our flight plan back in Recife."

Africa stretched out ahead as they flew on and on. The Ivory Coast, Nigeria, Angola, mist rising from Victoria Falls. Before reaching Salisbury (now Harare, in Zimbabwe), Clyde and Bob saw herds of wild elephants stampeding on the ground below.

At the Solusi Mission, they delivered the Cessna 185 flown by Bob. Together in the 182, they went on to Malamulo Mission. At a dedication service for the new plane, they invited Bob Seamount to speak.

"For me it's the dream of a lifetime to be able to deliver a plane to Malamulo," Seamount said. As a small boy I wanted a little red wagon more than anything else. My parents were poor, so I worked and saved for my wagon. Every time I earned some money, I gave my tithe and offering and put the rest in a little bank to go toward the red wagon.

"When I was about to buy the wagon, a missionary visited my church. He told how God blessed the work at the Malamulo Leper Hospital and how Malamulo Mission needed funds to expand its work. After the meeting I went home, opened my bank, and brought the money back to the church. I gave it all for Malamulo. No red wagon for me—Malamulo Mission and God's work were more important. Now that I've seen your mission, I know that was one of the best investments I ever made. I thank God for the privilege of joining you in dedicating your new mission plane. May it serve as a tool to help you win many for Christ."

"Bob," Clyde said as they prepared to leave, "you've just helped me understand why you gave some of the best years of your life to mission aviation in the Upper Amazon Mission of Peru. Since boyhood, you've been putting others first."

The flight with Bob, ferrying planes over the Atlantic to Africa, increased Clyde's faith in God. When all the bills were paid, including the airline tickets home, it had cost just $2,300 per plane. Each mission saved more than $7,500 and received their planes much sooner than if they had shipped them as ocean freight.

CHAPTER FIFTEEN

SAVAGE FIRE

B ack home with his family at the air base in Peru, Clyde
learned about a Chayawita Indian who suffered from a
dreadful skin disease. When Juan and his wife arrived at
Panán, the Doñez family took them into their home. The man's
condition grew progressively worse.

Clyde saw Juan on his next trip to the Panán mission station. The sick man had all the symptoms of savage fire, one of
the worst diseases in the Amazon. Small eruptions break out all
over the body causing severe itching and burning. The victim
scratches 24-hours a day, never getting relief from the pain.

Returning to the base, Clyde consulted the doctor at the
Yarina Cocha Hospital. "It's a difficult disease," he said, "but I
think I can help the man. I'd like to try."

Clyde took the new *Fernando Stahl* to get Juan. "How could
you take this pitiful man into your home?" he asked Pastor
Doñez. "He's such a horrible mess, I almost hate to take him in
the plane."

Immediately on arriving at Pucallpa, the Peters transported
him to the hospital for treatment. At the end of three months, the
doctor, pleased with his patient's progress, contacted the air base.
"Juan doesn't need to be hospitalized any longer. Could you keep
him at the base and just let him come in every day for treatment?"

Eleanor helped Clyde fix a place for Juan to stay in the
hangar. Seeing his new home, the patient's face turned into one
wide smile. His skin appeared clean and smooth and he didn't
scratch any more since his body didn't itch. He felt well and at-

tended Sabbath services every week at the air base church. Each day he walked to the hospital for another treatment.

After six weeks the doctor said, "Juan, I believe you're well. Tell the mission pilot you've recovered and are ready to go home to your family."

Arriving at Panán, Clyde showed the patient to Augusto Doñez. "Look, he's a new man." Juan's wife cried with joy when she saw her husband's clear skin.

While Juan was away getting treatment, the local church members had built a small thatched hut for his family. Delighted to be home, he helped his wife cultivate a garden and joined her in attending baptismal classes. Following many months of Bible study, Juan and his wife were baptized in the Paranapura River.

Weeks later on a hot humid afternoon, as Juan sat in front of his hut, he unconsciously started scratching. His wife observed ugly eruptions reappearing all over his body. Augusto dispatched an Indian to Balsa Puerto with instructions to send a telegram requesting the mission plane.

Clyde recoiled at the sight of a man who seemed to be well just a few months before, but he helped Juan into the aircraft. "Savage fire has to be the worst disease I've seen," he told Augusto. He took Juan back to the hospital and then lost contact with him.

Eleanor looked at her husband one morning. "Do you feel OK, Clyde?" she asked.

"Not really. My head aches and I feel hot." His wife brought a thermometer and found that his temperature was 103°. Still running a fever after several days in bed, she took him to the hospital. Doctors did many kinds of tests without determining the problem.

Juan, the Chayawita, in the same hospital, appeared to be doing better. He spent many hours in front of Clyde's room where he'd look in, wave, and smile. Doctors finally diagnosed Clyde as having a relapse from a previous bout with typhoid fever. After they provided the right medications, he recuperated and went home in a few days.

In the meantime, Juan got worse. The old eruptions appeared again and he scratched with both his hands all day long as he fought to find relief. The doctor asked the people at the air base to come for Juan. "We've done all we can," the physician said. "Huge doses of cortisone helped control the savage fire, but the side effects have ravaged his body. He will die and we can't keep him any more."

The staff at the air base repaired a small thatched hut near the hangar to provide Juan a place to stay. Three times a day Eleanor carried food to the suffering man. In spite of severe pain, he never failed to accept her kindness with words of appreciation.

Clyde's busy flight schedule servicing schools and missions didn't leave time for him to stop and visit the Indian. Around 10:00 one evening he heard a loud knock on their door. "Juan needs to see you," a messenger said. "He wants you to come right now."

"Why now?" Clyde asked. "I'm tired and have to leave on an early morning flight." Then sorry for what he had just said, he took a flashlight and walked to Juan's shack.

Juan spoke with difficulty, "Brother Peters, I want you to forgive me for anything I've done wrong. I've been a nuisance around the air base. I appreciate what you and Mrs. Peters have done for me."

Clyde felt a warm trickle of tears. "Forgive you? I need to ask you to forgive me." Peters stood there in the darkness with the humble Indian. "You haven't done a thing to ask forgiveness for. I just wish there was something we could do to help you get well. I should have come to visit you."

Clyde prayed with the Chayawita, then told him good night. Two days later Juan died. Peters' father, visiting the air base at the time, helped dig Juan's grave. After returning from a mission trip, Clyde learned of the funeral.

"I thought I was too busy to spend more time with Juan. Alone, unable to talk with his family, he knew he was dying and called for me. He wanted to be sure all his sins were forgiven. In my heart and mind he was a nuisance. I didn't like having him around the air base all the time. But I'm glad he let me pray with him before he died. He may not have understood all the doctrines, but he knew Jesus."

Clyde scheduled a flight to notify Juan's wife of her husband's death. "I want you to know," he told the woman, "your husband was the kind of man our family would like to spend eternity with."

One day Clyde and Eleanor went to bed early, but he could not sleep.

"Clyde, why are you staying awake?"

"I'm not worried about anything, Eleanor, but I should have gone to the dentist on my last trip to Lima. I've got a gnawing toothache that won't go away."

"Is there anything I can do?"

"Not really. At least not tonight." He was silent a moment. "Eleanor, can you believe that during our 10 years in the Amazon jungle, I've pulled nearly 40,000 teeth."

"I know you've pulled a lot."

"One day a woman came with her whole face swollen. I cringed when I looked in her mouth. After pulling nine teeth, I got nauseated watching a cup of puss pour out from where the teeth had been."

"Did her mouth heal OK?"

"Several weeks later I flew back to her village. She was fine and asked me to pull five more teeth. I've noticed that people like this woman, who live along the rivers where sugar, white flour and candy are part of the diet, have severe dental problems."

"What about the remote areas?"

"Indians in primitive areas, where no refined foods are available, have teeth like pearls."

In the morning Clyde's tooth still ached. "Eleanor," he said, "I've got to do something. My wisdom tooth's so far gone I'm going to lose it. The pain is more than I can stand. Let me show you how to give the injection and I'll pull it myself."

Eleanor's hand shook when she held the hypodermic needle in front of his nose. "Boy, you're really scared," he almost laughed. "I shouldn't have talked you into this."

Still shaking, she stuck the needle in the spot he showed her. Soon it felt numb. Clyde looked in the mirror, checking to make sure he had the forceps on the right tooth. When he rolled it back and forth, it popped right out, bringing him instant relief.

Eleanor didn't feel comfortable giving injections, but she loved teaching her children and they could not have had a better teacher than their own mother. Now it was time for academy and college. "Lord, help us to do the right thing for our children," the couple prayed.

CHAPTER SIXTEEN

SKYDIVERS FROM SPACE

After serving 10 years in the upper Amazon jungle of Peru, the Peters moved back to the United States where their children could complete their education. Settling near Union College in Lincoln, Nebraska, Shelly and Linda both became nurses. Alan mastered the building trade.

Clyde's parents were getting older. Although he could have managed the family farm, his heart still had wings. He flew for a medical group and performed occasional flights for the Mid-America Union and Union College. Besides serving on the Aviation Council for the North American Division, he made several flights taking Bibles to Russia.

When Melvin Peters developed prostate cancer, the family sold the farm and Mom and Dad Peters moved into an apartment adjoining Clyde's home. The cancer spread to his bladder. It had gone too far for surgery to be beneficial. Melvin lost a lot of blood and they took him to the hospital where he received multiple blood transfusions.

Late one afternoon Dr. Sorenson spoke briefly with Georgianna. "We've done all we can for your husband. He's going to die. Since you're a nurse, why don't you just take him home and keep him as comfortable as possible. We'll send home care nurses to help you."

Melvin loved it when daughter Joyce and his son-in-law came to visit. He liked being with Clyde and daughter-in-law Eleanor and most of all with his wife, Georgianna. To make him more comfortable she put an egg-crate mattress on his bed. He relished the healthy food she prepared and seemed to grow stronger.

One day he sat on the couch when his son came home in a helicopter. When Clyde offered to take Joyce for a helicopter ride, he announced, "I'm going, too!"

"Should we take Dad?" Joyce asked her brother.

"Sure, it'll be good for him." Brother and sister helped their father into the chopper and got him buckled up. Clyde started the engine, rotors began to whirl, and Dad smiled. "Son, you're the best pilot."

"Thank you, Dad."

As he flew Clyde remembered how as a teenager his father had protested his idea of his learning to be a pilot. "This flying business is just a waste of time," he had said. "I want you to grow up and run the farm." But the conflict over flying ended the day Clyde accepted the request to be the first official full-time mission pilot ever hired by the General Conference of Seventh-day Adventists. His father and mother supported his mission projects in every possible way. They gave donations as well as visited him and helped with work at the base and out on the mission stations. And they never complained when the *Fernando Stahl* went down in the river at Amaquería.

Melvin Peters enjoyed every moment of the helicopter flight around Lincoln and out over the area farms. When he continued to feel better, Joyce went home. He didn't receive any more transfusions and with the medications, he felt no pain. One evening Melvin prayed with Georgianna as he did every morning and night, then went to sleep.

Georgianna woke up at 3:00 a.m. and found Melvin sitting up in bed. She held a stethoscope to his chest. His heart skipped beats. At 6:00 a.m. Clyde came into the apartment to check on his father. "Dad doesn't seem well," his mother said.

Placing strong arms under his father, Clyde lifted him. "Maybe Dad had a stroke." Melvin Peters leaned forward and took a long, deep breath—his last.

The sheriff came to certify the death. Later he phoned Georgianna. "You took such good care of him. He's been in bed for months and there's not a sore on his body." The local undertaker released the body for transport to a mortuary in Kansas.

Clyde's hero, H.M.S. Richards, Sr., Voice of Prophecy founder, died the same day. The Junior Voice of Prophecy lessons Clyde had studied as a youngster completely changed the direction of the Peters family's lives. The gospel to all the world became their passion and mission.

While Clyde hurried to get a plane ready, Eleanor drove her mother-in-law to the airport, while the undertaker took the body. With the help of his son, Alan, Clyde gently placed his father's body in the plane. Tears flowed down his face as he turned the ignition and started the engine. Speeding down the runway, the plane lifted off, heading back to his boyhood home. He couldn't help thinking, *This is not Dad's last flight. He's been looking for Jesus to come. I must be faithful and see Dad again. Christ will come and one of those angel skydivers will pick Dad up and take him back to the cloud with Jesus.*

Four hours after Melvin Peters died, his son delivered him to the Goodland, Kansas, mortuary. That afternoon they arranged for the funeral to be held the next day—Friday, the preparation day. The town of Goodland, Kansas, nearly closed down for the funeral. Almost everyone came. Bob Nash sang one of Melvin's favorite hymns: "How Great Thou Art."

A few days after burying his father, Clyde made a helicopter flight to Ft. Collins, Colorado. On the way home he landed at the cemetery where his father had been buried. Warm tears flowed down his cheeks as he knelt beside the grave and prayed.

"Dear Lord, forgive me for the times I didn't treat my dad the way he deserved. Forgive me for failing to always honor You. Make me the man You want me to be. Help me to be a good father and husband. And help me to always share my faith in You. Bless Your work in the jungles of Peru. Keep me ready for Your coming, the resurrection, and a flight through space with Jesus."

After the Peters left the Amazon air base other missionary pilots continued reaching out to the tribes, but, more and more, terrorists plagued Peru. Twenty-five years after Clyde landed for the first time at the jungle air base, government authorities placed the Peruvian jungle under martial law. Terrorist attacks increased, making it dangerous to fly to remote outposts.

It saddened Clyde and Eleanor when they learned the last pilot had left and the airplanes were sold. Without planes to transport personnel, many churches and schools would be left without teachers and pastors. The Peters prayed that God would help the Indian members to remain faithful. They believed God would not abandon His true followers.

A letter from mission president, Lucio Calle, reported that "except for children too young for baptism, 100 percent of those who live in Amaquería are now baptized church members. They miss visits by the mission plane, but the work has grown."

One day a band of Shining Path guerrillas marched into Amaquería and demanded that the believers join them in their fight to take over the government of Peru. "Your women and children can work in the *chacras* raising coca plants for producing cocaine." The guerrilla movement used the drug traffic to help finance their revolution. "The men must carry arms and fight with us," they continued.

The Shipibo Indians resisted, insisting they must serve God. "We love Jesus. He doesn't want us to kill. Nor does He want us to break the laws of our country and be involved in the drug traffic. Because we worship God and keep His Sabbath, we will not join with you."

Angered, the guerrillas demanded, "Join with us or we'll kill you." But at the risk of their lives, the Amazon Christians stood firm in their decision to be true to Jesus.

One dark, moonless night, a group of terrorist guerrillas sneaked silently along under jungle cover toward Amaquería. They planned to keep their promise to kill everyone. As they were about to enter the village, the sound of airplane engines frightened them.

They knew it was against the law for private and commercial planes to fly over this part of the jungle at night. "It's Peru's air force!"their leader shouted. "They're looking for us."

Searching the sky, they saw a large plane, all lit up, and dozens of paratroopers with spotlights floating down toward the jungle. At the sight of men coming out of the night sky with parachutes, the startled guerrillas fled back into the darkness of the jungle.

After waiting a few weeks; they then returned, intent on destroying the *Adventistas* who refused to cooperate in spreading terror. Entering the village, they saw a bright light in the thatched church. Armed Peruvian soldiers marched out. "Where did these soldiers come from?" the terrorists cried. Afraid for their own lives, the guerrillas raced back into the jungle.

Still determined to massacre the faithful Shipibos, they returned in daylight. Everyone at Amaquería had gone out to work on their *chacras*. Finding the village empty, the guerrillas ransacked homes, taking everything of value. They left by a different route and walked into a Peruvian army ambush. All but three of the 40 Shining Path guerrillas died in the bloody battle that followed.

The three who escaped fled back to Amaquería. They told the villagers who had returned from their farms, "We came two times at night to kill every man, woman, and child in this village. First, a plane dropping men with parachutes thwarted us. On our next attempt we ran away when we saw soldiers with a bright light coming out of your church. When we came back today—the village was empty. Three times we've been foiled in our plans to exterminate you. How did you get the air force and then the army to protect you? What made you leave the village today?"

"No airplane has ever flown over our village dropping parachute jumpers at night," the Shipibo Indian believers said quietly. "The brightest light we have is a candle, and we've never had soldiers in our church."

"We're not telling you a story," the guerrillas insisted. "We saw this with our own eyes."

"If you saw paratroopers, they were God's skydivers from space. And if there were soldiers, it's like in the days of Elisha when God sent angels to protect His people."

One guerrilla, impressed with God's protection for Christians at Amaquería, stayed and studied the Bible. He believes angels had something to do with him getting out of the ambush alive when 37 others died. Today he is a baptized member of the Seventh-day Adventist Church.

Peru's current government has the founder of the Shining Path behind bars. The Tupac Amaru terrorists are under control. The government has lifted martial law and it's safe to travel in the jungle. Peters, eager to see the gospel reach every tribe in Peru, initiated the Peru Project. He joined with Maranatha and Adventist World Aviation in renovating the old air base. They put a new roof on the hangar, repaired the pilots' homes, and made dozens of other improvements. With the help of the Quiet Hour and the Piedmont Park Church, they raised funds and bought a used Cessna 182. Aided by others, Clyde overhauled the engine and refurbished the plane, making it like new. The ASI Convention held in Alburquerque, New Mexico, in August 1997 dedicated it as the *James J. Aitken*.

Most important, Peters trained Alberto Marín, the first

Peruvian to serve as a mission pilot. Clyde spent 100 hours helping Alberto learn the skills of a bush pilot, skills he would need in order to take off and land on short jungle strips under all kinds of conditions. Together the two men flew the *James J. Aitken* to Peru. The Amazon aviation ministry continues and every year Clyde takes groups to Peru to help with mission projects.